Turning Ten
Great Adventures in the Great Lakes

Second Edition

The true story of four outdoor adventures
made by ten-year-old children with their father
in the Great Lakes region.

Dan Ellens

Dedication

For Nick, Angie, Lyla and Kirk

Acknowledgments
Second Edition

I have had the good fortune to be able to live some of my childhood dreams as an adult, and to share those dreams with our children. Certainly, none of this would have been possible without the support of Cathy, my wife. I sincerely thank her for, not only helping to make each adventure possible, but also for encouraging me to write a home-spun account of each trip, and now, in 2022, for encouraging me to write a kind of Turning Ten epilogue.

The events in this book took place over a period of seven years. During that time, numerous people contributed in various ways. In addition, many people along the path of each adventure gave their local advice, or shared their hospitality, helping to make our trips a joy. My appreciation for those whose help led to the first edition has been acknowledged in the original book.

Since then, I have been inspired by Dave and Jan Heaven whom we met on the waters of Lake Huron during Kirk's kayaking adventure. Dave's correspondence has helped to anchor my view of the wilds, and to confirm the important place the wilds take in family life.

Judd and Cathryn Kaiser's Turning Ten story has also been an inspiration illuminating the relevance of an update to the original book.

I thank all of the people who read the 2000 edition of _Turning Ten – Great Adventures in the Great Lakes_, many of whom now have their own journal sitting on a shelf in their home, documenting an adventure taken with their child or grandchild. I thank those who wrote to me after their adventures, to let me know that their child had recently joined the _Turning Ten Club_.

Contents

Second Edition Reflections
A 2022 Epilogue

Lyla leaned against the fence, a common border defining the south side of her yard and the north side of her neighbor's property. Her own small children played in the grass behind her. Cathryn, Lyla's neighbor, leaned against the fence also and chatted while looking over her shoulder at Judd, her husband. He was leaving their barn carrying a cedar strip canoe, which he had built himself, heading for the roof of a car parked further down their driveway. Cathryn noticed Lyla's curiosity.

"Oh, Judd and the children built that canoe. We used it in every one of the kids' turning ten trips."

"Turning ten?" Lyla asked, somewhat surprised.

"Yes, each time one of our children turned ten years old, Judd took them for several days on an outdoor adventure. It really is amazing. Lots of people are doing it. There is even a man who wrote a book about the *Turning Ten* idea."

Lyla, with even more surprise, "Really? You're kidding?"

"Not at all. You and Kevin should think about it. All of our children have loved their chance. It has been one of their main events while growing up."

"Really? Do you happen to have the book?"

"Of course. Let me get it."

Lyla's heart beat faster. "It couldn't be," Lyla thought as Cathryn walked to her house and emerged a few minutes later with a large white book in her hand.

Lyla cautiously took the book, as if being reunited with an old friend. She gently thumbed through the pages until reaching Chapter 3, *'Teamwork on a Tandem with a Ten-Year-Old, A Ride Across Michigan...Lyla'*.

Cathryn's eyes widened. "Is that you? You are serious? I have got to tell Judd."

Later that day, as the sun was setting, Cathy and I joined Lyla's family and her neighbors at a backyard campfire. We were all laughing, and talking, and watching the fireflies. Judd suddenly looked across the fire. "You know, Dan, this is not the first time we've met."

"Hmm, I just cannot place it."

"It was about fifteen years ago. You were in downtown Plymouth doing a book signing. I walked into the bookstore wearing a Tilley hat, with four small children in tow. You stood up, reached across the table, and placed your hand on my arm. You said, "If anyone could use this book, it is you." I bought the book. It really inspired me, and our children. I wanted to let you know and to thank you tonight."

Later in the week Judd showed me his hand-built canoe, a similar cedar strip kayak, and an armful of hand-built paddles. Each child received a paddle as a birthday gift in advance of their Turning Ten adventure. Judd told me that three of his work colleagues had also followed along in the tradition. His granddaughter will have her turning ten trip this coming summer. All of it warmed my heart.

Judd and son, Haydn, on a Turning Ten adventure

It has now been 22 years since writing *Turning Ten – Great Adventures in the Great Lakes*. During that time the book has touched me in many unexpected ways. A colleague who borrowed Kirk's kayak to take a trip with his young grandson after reading the book. A boy scout troop whose membership each purchased a copy of the book. An invitation to speak to a group of fathers who were interested to know how the experiences had impacted our children. A reader who visited Isle Royale with his family after reading the book. I am still periodically contacted by people whom I have never met, who want to let me know that they recently read the book and duplicated one of the trips, or did something similar with their own child, or with their grandchild.

A few months ago, at a large family reunion, my cousin's husband, Piet, pulled up a chair next to me. "You're the one who got me in so much trouble," he said with a mixture of smile and concern on his face.

I was surprised. I had no idea what he was talking about.

"You wrote that book. I took a Turning Ten adventure with our two children. Then things got complicated," Piet laughed, "and I could never get organized for our third child's trip. He asks me every year about his Turning Ten time. He's almost 24 years old now, and still brings it up."

I chuckled, knowing Piet was teasing me, "I surrender."

A whole new generation is growing up since the book was first written. Some with their own children who they will take on an outward-bound adventure at ten years old because their parents did it with them. Others who have been told about the *Turning Ten Club* for the first time, and are planning their own adventures with their children. Much has changed since 1993 when Nick and I walked across Isle Royale together. Technological change seems to have touched every facet of outdoor recreation. Most gear is lighter, warmer, and more water-proof than what we used beginning three decades ago. Canoes and kayaks are less expensive. Bicycles are lighter with wider gear ranges. A whole network of safe new trails has been built. There are new hiking shoes, new energy snacks, new bug repellants, mobile phones, and cell signals all around.

It is the enticing aspects of technological progress that make Turning Ten adventures even more valuable today than a generation ago. As it becomes increasingly easy for children to entertain themselves in front of a mobile phone, a computer screen, or a television, many miss the hands-on experience with nature and the outdoor environment that their predecessors grew up experiencing, and perhaps taking for granted. Many children in today's world know facts about the natural world by engaging in their digital environment, but many have not had the chance to watch a live eagle soar through the sky, observe a bass hovering over its sandy nest in water at the edge of a pond, swim in a natural lake, build a campfire to warm their breakfast, or encounter that wake-up-in-the-woods experience. We are approaching a generation of children who may miss it because their parents missed it; whose parents simply do not know where to start. The good news is that parents can start almost anywhere, and their children will follow.

It is not only the connection with nature that has potential to enrich the lives of every generation of children, it is also the simple participation of a parent with their child in those making that connection. It is a parent-child opportunity that anyone can complete at their own pace, their own skill level, and in the context of their own physical ability. No one will judge. A Turning Ten adventure is just one venue for parental participation. What I like about it is the planning, the anticipation, the practice, the adventure, and finally, the challenge; an adventure and challenge as much for the parent as for the child.

This year Lyla's daughter turns ten years old. She and Kevin have already mapped out a 150-mile canoe journey on Michigan's Muskegon River. Their camp sites are roughly placed on the map. Their supplies are accumulating in the corner of a basement closet. Their home-built canoe paddles are 50% complete. Lyla's daughter will become another member of the *Turning Ten Club*. I am sure she will begin fifth grade knowing that she accomplished something extraordinary during her summer break, and that she will carry with her fond memories that last a lifetime, of the time spent with her father; memories that Kevin will also cherish.

It is 30 years since the first Turning Ten adventure. Perhaps, as I now approach my mid-60s, next summer I will again break into the now-busy lives of our adult children and, with each of them, visit a milestone spot from the trip that was their initiation into the *Turning Ten Club*. Together we will reflect on the many adventures that life, with its good fortune, has dropped in our laps.

Preface
2000

When our oldest son turned ten years old, like many children his age, he seemed to challenge every word we spoke. Each day included some things he must do, and then explanations about why the things to do were valid, and then negotiation about whether the things would be done. One day I stepped back from this situation and realized that I needed to do something different for a few days. I needed to spend a long stretch of one-on-one time with our son in an environment that would be productive in a different way; a time with less rules, heavy on self-discipline and light on regulation, heavy on partnering and light on parenting.

I mulled this over in my mind and discovered that it presented a great opportunity. Since I was a teenager, I had wanted to hike Isle Royale. I had been intrigued by the adventure a friend had made to the island with his father before his senior year of high school. But could a ten-year-old do it? I started to gather information. Looking at a map, I discovered that the island could be broken into several ten-mile segments. Could Nick walk ten miles in a day? One mile an hour for ten hours...I began to wonder if ten miles was far enough. The answer was obvious. With the energy level of a ten-year-old, the distance was really only a matter of perspective. If he could do it for one day, was there anything that would stop him from doing it for two? Three? So, I convinced myself that it could be done.

I liked the challenge of the trip, but also liked that the expedition would be in a completely safe environment. Our challenge was focused on endurance, not danger; the perfect combination for an adult and a child. It was a journey to a remote area, something not done every day. What I knew for sure was that such a trip could not take place without stirring up something unusual along the way, something that memories are made of.

So, it began.

When our oldest daughter turned ten, like many children her age would do, she immediately asked "What are we going to do for my trip?"

Fortunately, the question did not hit me blind. I had already taken equal time into consideration. I could see that this was truly an unbelievable excuse to plan some of the big adventures that I would have wanted to do as a teenager. Cathy and I have four children. That meant four trips; each with an outward-bound emphasis; each a physical challenge for any adult, but each doable by a ten-year-old.

These adventures were as much for me as for the children. We worked together on the planning and preparation, but the decision of location and format was up to me. No one objected. I wanted to give the children a feel for survival, an appreciation for the wilderness, a guaranteed sense of accomplishment and also a love for the Great Lakes region. In the end I hoped that they would walk away with an intuitive sense that they could take on something really big, if they did it one step at a time.

Angie's adventure was an extension of one of my fondest outdoor childhood memories. As early teenagers, my younger brother and I were invited to join family friends for two days of canoeing on the Au Sable River. Since then, the Au Sable has held an elevated status on my list of rivers. Imagine canoeing it from beginning to end! That's an even longer trek than the world-famous Au Sable River Marathon. I had never canoed a river from start to finish, but Angie's tenth year provided the perfect chance.

When Lyla turned ten, I wondered if we would have to break the trend. We were in the midst of a foreign assignment in Bangalore, India and the completion date was somewhat unclear. The assignment had already lasted more than 18 months and we wondered whether we would return in time to do Lyla's trip without delaying for one year.

Lyla's adventure would be bicycling, perhaps because during my mid-teenage years bicycle touring was my passion. In Michigan, the premier end point for any bicycle trip is Mackinac Island. So, we planned to travel under power of pedal from our home in Southeast Michigan to the northern tip of

Michigan's lower peninsula, where we could catch a ferry to the island.

While in India, we also wondered whether we would return with enough time for Lyla to improve her two-wheeler skills and build up the necessary muscles before the trip. Should I make another selection? Fortunately, we were back in the USA with one full season to learn to ride and another few months for toning.

Our change from individual bikes to a tandem with less than one month before the trip was a last-minute improvement. It was made for safety considerations more than any other reason. We would be riding the edge of the pavement, as is done in cycle touring, which meant that there was always the potential of motor vehicles close by. A single wrong move by Lyla on her own bike under those conditions was too dangerous for my liking. So, I was in control of the front handlebars, and she provided the pedal power. That was a fair arrangement for me. Our somewhat unusual route was based on two factors, campground spacing, and rural, low traffic roads. Safety first!

The following June Kirk turned ten. At the time of his trip he was the youngest of the bunch, five months younger than Angie was when her trip occurred. The venue for Kirk's expedition was chosen somewhat by default. The other children had already hiked, biked and canoed. Kayaking was one thing that was still left undone.

Kirk's adventure was something new for both of us. We had not been in a sea kayak before, but I imagined that this type of craft was simply a sophisticated version of a canoe...with which I had plenty of experience. We had no experience with open water, but my rationale was that if we stayed a few yards from shore, the worst thing that could happen would be to capsize and swim to land. I was sure that once we got a few miles under our belts we would have a good feel for how far we could venture without being unsafe. During our eighty-mile trip we never made a move in the kayak that we were not comfortable with. We never placed ourselves in a situation that we couldn't have handled if we had capsized. As it turned out, our comfort level increased as we went, and by the third day, when the waves were nearly five feet, we felt completely at ease with our vessel.

At the end of it all, each of our children has something to remember the trip by. The tent used for all four trips now belongs to Nick, along with an adult size backpack. Angie has a Grumman canoe that she can make her own expeditions in. Lyla gets the tandem bicycle when she has room to store it, and Kirk will keep the kayak.

For me, in the corner of our bedroom I keep the walking stick that I made for Nick's trip, with a trout carved in its shaft. Next to it, there is a canoe paddle I built for Angie's journey, with a fly fisherman carved on the handle. Hanging from the strap on the walking stick are the bicycling gloves that I used with Lyla. And this summer I added a beautiful 240 cm wooden *Tail Wind* kayak paddle to the corner.

People have asked, "What's next?"

We really do have a plan. But this time it is Cathy's turn. After studying German in school for three years, when Nick turned sixteen, he spent one week in Germany with Cathy. Angie has been studying French and will turn sixteen this year. They will visit France. The younger two haven't started a language yet, but they know the program, and Kirk has already asked what the principal language of Antarctica is.

My original intent for creating the stories in this book was to preserve memories. I hoped that someday each child would pick up the photo album, find the story, and remember with fondness what they had done.

After completing three of the trips, I realized that the stories could be more than that. In offering them as book, my goal is to inspire other parents and children to spend some time like this together. If you do, your children will feel like superheroes, and you may too.

Each trip in this book is possible to duplicate. Given time, I would do any of them again. I am sure, however, that you will have more fun planning your own adventure from scratch. These kinds of trips need not be expensive, although each of our trips seemed to consume more funds than the previous one. I can say without reservation that the money was well spent, and the benefits went far beyond the investment.

Each of our children became genuinely excited about their sibling's upcoming adventure. It was as if one by one they were joining a club; the *Turning Ten Club*. They each knew that their own time would come when they would complete a challenge that would give them the right of membership. With all four on the roster, it is impossible for me to enter our bedroom without seeing the walking stick, gloves and paddles in the corner, and thinking of the thrilling times the children and I spent together.

Enjoy the stories.

Chapter One

Isle Royale

Trailing A Ten-Year-Old Across
Isle Royale

Nick

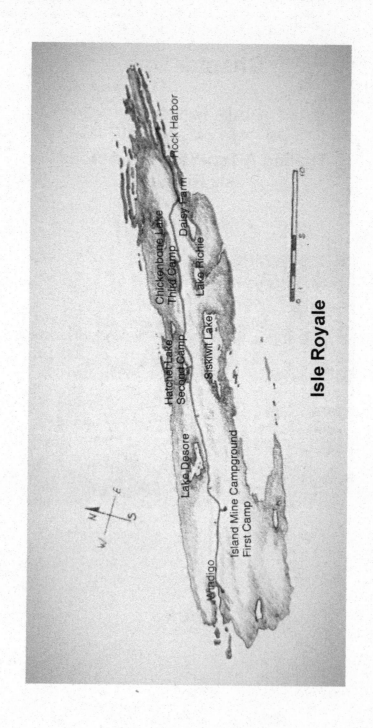

Isle Royale

After two days we saw our first moose. Having passed numerous marshy bogs and miles of deep forest, seeing the dark creature out in the open at the top of one of the island's highest and rockiest peaks caught us by surprise. Such is the magic of Isle Royale. A hike of almost 50 miles carrying a full pack is a task many adults might avoid, let alone a ten-year-old boy. But the chance of four nights alone in the woods with his father was like an opportunity to explore a new frontier. We had already heard a wolf howl in the night and had listened to squirrels and foxes scamper about outside of our tent in the dark. Although we had read stories of Isle Royale and were briefed by friends who made the trip before, nothing short of being there could have prepared us for the grandeur of the Isle Royale experience.

Our adventure began almost ten months earlier when Nick received a junior-size backpack on his tenth birthday. We spent the next few months picking up supplies, and making plans to tackle a five-day trip on foot in one of North America's most remote wilderness areas. In June we each cut a limb from a hickory tree and whittled it down for a custom fitted walking stick. We removed bark from the sticks and carved our names into them, finishing them with sandpaper and varnish. In the final weeks we practiced hiking, at first filling our packs with books, and finally packing our actual supplies. People waved from their cars when they saw us, a young boy and a full-grown man, walking down the country roads with full packs. All the while we imagined what this mysterious island would be like and how we would fare in its crossing.

I could see the thrill on Nick's face as we boarded the five-passenger seaplane. The pilot stuffed gear into every available niche in the tiny airplane. He made jokes about the full canteens as he loaded them into the plane, and halfheartedly threatened to charge us fifty dollars for the extra weight. The other two passengers could see that we had not transported gear in a small seaplane before. Their canteens were empty. By early afternoon the plane was safely tied to the dock at Windigo, Isle Royale's western outpost, and we were buying stove fuel at the small camp store. The ground we stood on was as foreign to our lifestyle as an undiscovered continent. It was a land without the conveniences of telephones, fast moving cars, supermarkets, or medical facilities; a land of quietness, loneliness, tranquility and self-sufficiency.

The inhabitants of this patch of earth are not the rangers or hikers, for they are merely caretakers and guests. The residents are the moose, perhaps 1600 in all, the timber wolf, though at the time of our trip they may have numbered less than ten, beavers, foxes, loons, squirrels, eagles, bats and countless other creatures who struggle for survival in this home with a Lake Superior address. Hoping to be houseguests of the moose and wolves, we hitched up our backpacks and headed east the full length of the island.

We walked little more than half a mile before entering the deep maple forest that was to shield us from sunlight for more than a day. It was as if we had entered a cave where the surroundings were damp from a summer without sun. Thimbleberries grew in thick patches, providing a soft mask to the rugged island floor. Only the path exposed the bare ground. It was obvious how quickly this opening through the foliage could revert into jungle-like vegetation, if not for the foot traffic that kept it in check. In low marshy areas, single board bridges stretched across wet spots. Moose tracks on either side of the planks made me wonder whether human or beast was first to break the trail.

Our mission was to follow the Greenstone Ridge Trail down the backbone of the island for about three and a half days. From there we intended to cut south to the Lake Superior shore and follow the island coast eastward to the town of

Rock Harbor. Nick led the way, at first stubbing his toe on every root and rock in the trail. As time went by, his walking style adapted on its own to avoid the small obstacles at ground level. When my turn came to lead, we encountered the first plank bridge over a low area. I walked across, pushing low branches aside to clear the way. As the first branch swung back, I heard a loud yelp from Nick. I quickly looked over my shoulder and found Nick lying on his back, on his pack, in the swamp grass like a turtle turned over on its shell. The branch had connected with his mid-section, picked him off the ground, and launched him into the brush. Keeping score, that was one for the island and zero for the hiking team. Hoping we could keep the score close for the rest of the journey, I turned that wiggling turtle back onto his feet and we pushed forward.

We knew that if we were going to be successful on this trip, we would have to pace ourselves. We planned each day's destination, estimating our food requirements and the amount of water we needed to carry between spots where our supply could be replenished. Our practice hikes had established a predictable rate of about two miles per hour while we were walking. Now we walked for half an hour at a time. We took breaks whether we needed them or not. After the first half hour we stopped for 5 minutes - and savored two mouthfuls of water. We walked another half hour and stopped for 15 minutes. This time we dipped into our trail mix or ate a piece of jerky. Two more swallows of water were again a welcomed reward. We repeated the sequence time after time and managed to cover seven miles to our evening destination.

Nick set up the tent while I began to boil water for soup and coffee. I pumped water through our purifier from a small stream close by. We were deep in the heart of a vast maple forest. The canopy overhead let isolated rays of light pass through to ground level, like lasers pointing to a leaf here, or a rock there, or perhaps pinpointing a hollow opening in a tree inhabited by some small animal. We felt truly isolated. Only three people crossed our trail on the day's hike. While one other small tent with two hikers was pitched in the camp area, on the trail it was as if we had the island to ourselves. Over the next 30 miles we encountered only three more humans.

Breaking camp at 7:30 a.m., our most difficult day lay ahead. We intended to hike nearly 14 miles to Hatchet Lake, a walk the ranger had not recommended for a ten-year-old with a 20-pound pack. "Why not eat all the food in our packs now so they aren't so heavy?" Nick joked as we considered our day's walk. Just before noon we finally broke out of the woods to find a scenic lookout over Lake Desore and an open view all the way to Thunder Bay, Ontario. Our walking sticks clicked in rhythm as the trail crossed huge rocks marked by occasional cairns placed to show the way. We napped on a rock in the sun after lunch, feeling the warm rays upon our faces. The ridges we were traversing were the highest of the island.

With the new terrain, it seemed as though we had moved to another island. Our feet landed on an unforgiving rock surface, rather than a soft trail made from centuries of decaying foliage. From the dark humid jungle, we had traveled to a rocky desert. We took a break out in the open and felt the relief of having the packs off our backs.

As we sat and talked about the view, the sudden sound of a breaking limb came from the trees. Another branch crunched. Then another. The slow methodical noise of a creature moving through the brush pulled us to attention. We crept to the edge of the woods hoping for a glimpse. I felt my heart pound, as we got closer. A shadow drifted though the birch trees. The beast was huge. It moved like a ghost unaware of our presence. The animal looked so unusual; its head arranged in a strange formation of cheeks, lips and ears, like a sad-faced circus clown intended to inspire laughter in children and adults. Nick and I looked at each other and chuckled when the moose turned to see us. We could see a strange grin pass across the creature's face, and as suddenly as the moose had appeared, it vanished into the shadows of the birch forest.

We were both worn out by the time we reached our campsite at Hatchet Lake. We walked along like zombies, each step bringing us closer to our goal. As a ten-year-old will, Nick sensed a rare opportunity. He began to ask innocent questions to which I answered, "yes" as if in a trance. He decided to turn it up a notch. "When we get home may I have a sleep over party?"

"Yes."

"Can I invite ten friends?"

"Yes.".

"Fifteen?"

"Yes."

"Will you increase my allowance next week?"

"Yes...."

I'm sure that I would have tripled his allowance and agreed to let him drive across Michigan's Upper Peninsula if he had continued to ask. Fortunately, perhaps by an act of God, I was saved by a small wooden monument that identified Hatchet Lake and pointed us toward the camping area.

It is incredible how quickly a body adjusts to a more disciplined lifestyle and how good the change actually feels. We were up and eating oatmeal by 6 a.m., never eating our fill, but eating as much as our supply would allow. This day our packs felt comfortable on our shoulders. We knew that we would have more time to take in the surroundings since our goal was only ten miles from Hatchet Lake. When we made camp, a quarter mile hike brought us down to Chickenbone Lake for a swim and some fishing. We really weren't set up for pike, the prize fish of Isle Royale, but I put a fly rod in Nick's hands with hopes that he would catch some smaller trout. He stood waist deep in water casting the line like a pro, while I watched the loon behind him drifting about in the middle of this beautiful lake.

During the night it rained steadily from midnight until 4 a.m. I remembered tent technology from when I was a boy. I believe tent floors were the new things at that time. The tents I was used to were the military variety. They were not light, and rain flies were definitely not available. Now I lay in our tent in the rain. The tent weighed slightly more than 4 pounds, including the rain fly. We were dry. Completely dry. I was impressed.

We began our hike again the next morning. While it wasn't actually raining, everything was wet. Water dripped off the trees. The grass was covered with water. The ground was wet. Before we knew it, we were wet. The water completely changed the look of the landscape. A heavy fog hung near tree level. It produced an eerie feeling that muffled our senses. The acute definition of sight and sound were dampened into a mystic blur. We cautiously walked around each bend, wondering what strange thing we would encounter. For Nick, the rain was a new experience. It showed him one more element of survival in the wild.

The fourth day would be another long one. We expected to pull into Rock Harbor campground early in the evening after covering almost 14 miles. Traveling east for several miles on the Greenstone Ridge Trail we intercepted a southbound path that brought us to the Daisy Farm Campsite on Lake Superior's shore. As we started our final seven miles into Rock Harbor, people who had only left the ferry several hours earlier began crossing our trail. We felt a bit triumphant knowing that now we were the veteran hikers. When other hikers passed, Nick and I intentionally walked a little straighter and faster to make it appear as if we knew what we were doing. As soon as the other hikers were out of sight Nick and I looked at each other and laughed, thinking that we had fooled them. But, having walked from one end of Isle Royale to the other, we knew in our hearts that we were no longer novices.

When we finally strode into town, we both felt two inches taller, for we had accomplished what we had planned to do more than ten months earlier. I don't know what made me feel better, knowing that I had actually done something I had wanted to do since I was a teen, or knowing that Nick had just accomplished a feat fit for any adult.

That evening Nick and I began to fade back into civilization. We paid $2.50 for a shower and ate a sit-down meal at the Rock Harbor Lodge restaurant. We sat at our table and talked until the restaurant closed, then watched the sun disappear before climbing back into our tent.

I awoke suddenly at 3:30 a.m., as if beckoned back by the wilds. My tired muscles felt satisfied but my spirit was restless. Looking at Nick, I noticed he was wide-awake too. We slipped into our hiking boots and quietly crawled out of the tent. The sky was perfectly clear and the stars were spectacular. We walked down the trail for a mile in the darkness to find a large rock that was clear of trees. Here we absorbed a final dose of Isle Royale's wild beauty. We lay on our backs and watched the stars - so many stars that it was hard to pick out the Big Dipper. Shooting stars zipped across the sky and, as if God had smiled at us, the Northern Lights began to dance on the horizon. I knew that I had finally been given everything I had come to Isle Royale for. Nick and I silently followed the path back to our tent. As I slipped back into my sleeping bag, I felt completely content. Closing my eyes, I wondered how this reality could mingle so effortlessly with my dreams.

As we took the ferry back to Michigan's Upper Peninsula, I watched Nick carry on conversations with rangers returning home from the summer on the island. I watched him walk around the ship on his own and buy his own food when he was hungry. It was as if he had grown two steps at once. I knew that when he returned to his first week of fifth grade, he would have some great stories to tell.

Chapter Two

The Au Sable River

Beaver Dams, Holy Water, and a Ten-Year-Old

Angie

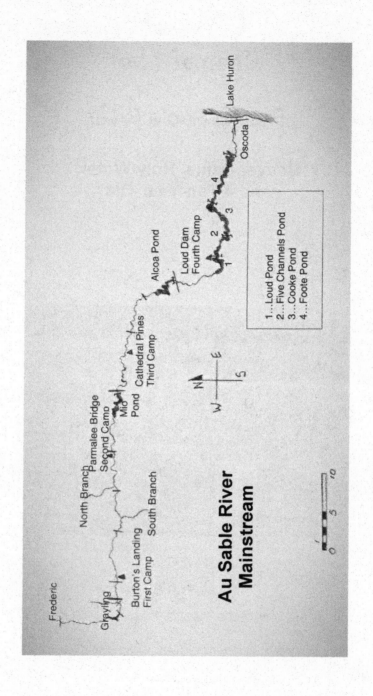

Au Sable River Mainstream

Frederic

Grayling

North Branch

Parmalee Bridge
Second Camp

Burton's Landing
First Camp

South Branch

Mio
Pond

Cathedral Pines
Third Camp

Alcoa Pond

Loud Dam
Fourth Camp

Oscoda

Lake Huron

1
2
3
4

1...Loud Pond
2...Five Channels Pond
3...Cooke Pond
4...Foote Pond

N
W   E
S

0   5   10

Holy Water is the name given by serious trout fishers to portions of Michigan's Au Sable River. When we launched our canoe in Frederic, we did so with a reverence for this special river. Five days later we pulled the canoe onto the beach of Lake Huron with a healthy respect for the river; a respect for the upper portions of the river between Frederic and Grayling, where the stream narrows to widths barely passable; a respect for expansive ponds created by the Au Sable's six permanent dams; and a respect for the final section of the river where an underwater forest of fallen timber adds obstructions and danger for the canoeist.

For almost a year Angie and I had planned the adventure that would take place during the summer after her tenth birthday. Our goal was to canoe the Au Sable from beginning to end. Anticipation built up slowly during the planning months. We bought a used 17-foot Grumman aluminum canoe in October, built our own paddles in December, gathered canoeing, camping, and fly-fishing supplies in June, and took a practice run down the Huron River in July. When early August finally arrived, we could hardly sit still. We loaded the canoe and gear onto our station wagon and drove to the northern region of Michigan's Lower Peninsula.

After a night in a Grayling hotel, we followed country roads to a small bridge at the southern edge of Frederic, one of Michigan's small rural towns. The road narrowed to one lane as it crossed this lonely bridge. When we lowered the canoe through the grassy roadside ditch onto the small gravely patch of riverbank, we felt an awkward contrast between the isolation of the river and the industrial hum of the vehicle still idling on the road's dusty shoulder. Our gear consisted of a large waterproof backpack, a mesh decoy bag filled with items that could get wet, a spare paddle attached to one side of the canoe interior with a bungee cord, and two fly rod cases tied to the opposite side of the canoe.

Angie buttoned up her life vest and we accepted a push into the current from Nick. Angie and I turned for a final wave goodbye to see Cathy and the three children wishing us Bon Voyage. I sunk my homemade paddle deep into the water for its first Au Sable stroke and immediately lodged the canoe on a genuine piece of Au Sable driftwood. There we sat in our vessel, fifteen feet from the bridge, stuck solidly in the Michigan wilderness. We looked back to see the good laugh we were giving our four cheerleaders on the bridge and adamantly refused Nick's offers to rescue us by walking over to push us off the obstruction. Wiggling ourselves loose, we swallowed our pride, and thanked God that we had taken the only camera with us in the canoe. I could only imagine what was going through Cathy's mind as we covered our second fifteen feet, knowing that we planned to traverse about 150 miles of riverbed in the next five days.

The following five hours brought us through sections of the river that were barely wide enough for the canoe to pass. Brush and fallen cedars reached in from the bank and it seemed as if a jungle would fold in to swallow up the river. Time after time we lay flat with our backs against the canoe, the only means of proceeding downstream as we passed under fallen branches that formed low passageways.

After less than ten miles we encountered our first beaver dam. It looked like a gigantic plate of spaghetti stretching across the stream. Water on the upstream side of the dam was two feet deeper than the swift moving downstream flow. As if we were a battering ram, we boosted our canoe to ramming speed and lodged its front end high up on the beaver dam. In front, Angie stepped onto the pile of sticks with visions of urging the canoe to the other side, complete with nearly 100 pounds of gear and a 200-pound human rudder in the rear. I knew I could help by both unloading the rudder and adding horsepower to the towing device. Easing myself out of the canoe, I found myself unexpectedly waist deep in dark, black silt with a nice twelve-inch layer of water that formed icing on top.

We used a different strategy to attack the next beaver dam. The river's terrain changed from mile to mile. An area unfolded of water meandering through a swampy meadow, making sharp U-turns back and forth across the open, grassy area. We were just settling into the peaceful nature of the stream when our course was suddenly interrupted by one hundred feet of stream congested at every point with driftwood stumps. Realizing that navigating through this obstacle course would be nearly impossible, I quickly jumped into the chest deep water to walk the canoe through the entanglement. Negotiating my grip from log to log, we wove through the current until we reached the final thirty feet of the log jam where we found a passable route only four feet wide that allowed us to ride our vessel to easier terrain. No sooner did we turn the next bend than we encountered a fallen tree, crossing the entire river like a bridge, with only one foot of clearance over the water. We both climbed into the river and yanked the canoe over the tree trunk. Such are the surprises of the Au Sable River.

Our goal for the day was to reach Burton's Landing, a canoe launch and campground. This spot is also the beginning of the main stream Au Sable's catch and release, flies only fishing area. Knowing we must first portage a small dam in Grayling, we began looking for the marshy back up that would lead to the dam. As we paddled around a bend, we noticed a small DNR sign on the riverbank: "Caution, deep water ahead." Not more than fifty feet downstream the river funneled into a narrow chute with concrete walls and made a quick downhill run, dropping about three feet in just a short distance. We pointed the canoe directly down the riffling water hill and shot into the large pool at the bottom, our best "white water" experience of the trip.

In just a short distance the river opened to the large swamp we had been looking for. Weather beaten stumps stood erect in the water like an army of grandfathers, showing remains of the original forest. A tall mast planted amongst the stumps with a platform at the top housed an eagle's nest constructed from sticks large enough that the same beavers who had barricaded the river ten miles upstream could have made it. An eagle, perched in a pine by the bank, watched us paddle past while a second eagle circled overhead.

When we reached the dam in Grayling, it took us nearly 45 minutes to portage our gear and the canoe across James Street, Grayling's main thoroughfare. I knew that we were not the first to interrupt the steady stream of traffic of this busy road. We were, however, probably strong contenders for transporting the most gear!

We launched the canoe again from the walkway next to Grayling's Fly Factory, into a river that was now wider and more easily traveled by novices like us. We felt a bit relieved with the new conditions and relaxed as we paddled this less difficult stretch of stream. The canoe glided quietly around each bend and we faded into a state of equilibrium with the river. In a sudden movement, with no warning at all, a fearsome creature reached its powerful arm up from the river bottom and grabbed the back of the canoe. The Au Sable River Monster, disguised as a single cedar root lurking below the water's surface, tried in one mighty motion to capsize the entire craft. Instead, it settled for throwing the captain of the vessel overboard into a neck deep hole inhabited mostly by sunken logs and huge brown trout - a token sacrifice for such a formidable monster. The captain, shocked that such a thing could happen to him, with wildly swinging arms managed to barely snag the canoe and both paddles before they could escape and avoid association with the source of embarrassment splashing around in the stream. Realizing now that the creature feeds primarily on the individual steering from the rear, it took Angie until noon the next day to work up the courage to pilot the canoe.

The campground at Burton's Landing was a welcome sight when we finally paddled up onto the riverbank at 7:00 p.m. We shuttled our gear to an attractive site and settled in for our first night on the river.

By 6:30 a.m. we were up again for a breakfast of oatmeal, coffee and hot chocolate. This second day brought us through the Holy Waters, a long segment of river where the water sparkles with riffles created by the river bottom below. The streambed is naturally paved with multi-colored stones ranging in size from golf balls to grapefruit. Trout call this place home, and we watched many of them rise to capture the tiny insects landing on the water surface. Using a fly rod for the first time, Angie cast a line back and forth from the canoe with a fly that Nick had tied for her. Before long she pulled in her first brook trout. I hoped that we would be back to the Holy Waters someday to wade the stream

and fish, without a need to reach a downstream goal.

We set up our tent at the Parmalee Bridge Campground and were again on the river by 8:00 a.m. This was a good day for spotting wildlife. We saw seven eagles, twelve deer, five mink, several beaver, and so many blue herons that we lost count. Kingfishers crisscrossed the river in front of our canoe for almost the entire day.

At noon we reached our first hydroelectric dam near Mio. A yellow canoe sign positioned at the top of a tall pole marked the portage spot. This was a marker we would look for throughout the rest of the trip, since Mio Dam was only the first of six large dams placed strategically along the river. We shuttled our gear from the still water at the top of the dam to the swift river below. We noticed the signs that warned: "Danger! when siren sounds leave the river immediately." It was a situation we did not want to experience. Only a short time after the alarm sounds the gates of the dam open, allowing a surge of water to rush from the reservoir above the dam. The water level can rise as much as three feet in the river from the sudden flow.

Au Sable is a name given to this river by French explorers. A DNR ranger translated it for us as meaning "all sand, or through the sand." As we paddled downstream it became obvious how this river was named, since at each bend a sand cliff raises high above the riverbed to an overlooking plateau. The ranger explained that on Cooke Dam Pond there is a set of stairs next to one of these huge, cliff-like sand dunes. If you count, you will find that there are 250 steps coming down the steep descent...and 500 returning up the same path; especially if you are carrying a backpack. When we eventually passed this spot, I knew exactly what he meant.

We made camp at a small, two-tent location called Cathedral Pines. From the water the spot is a gravel bank just large enough to pull up two canoes. A few steps up the trail the brush opens to a clearing canopied by towering pines. Near Oscoda, on the shores of Lake Huron, a foot trail begins called the Michigan Shore-to-Shore Riding and Hiking Trail. This path winds through the Huron National Forest, with Lake Michigan as its finishing point. On the east side of Michigan, the trail follows the Au Sable River, with campsites spaced close enough together to suit backpackers on foot. Cathedral Pines is one of these campsites, serving the dual purpose as a canoeing camp and a backpacking spot. The Shore-to-Shore Trail, the campsite's only land access, runs directly through the center of the main clearing.

Our canoe was in the river by 8:30 a.m. and we began a day of paddling that would bring us through a long winding portion of river to a large modern campground on the north side of Alcona Dam Pond. The morning presented an abundance of wildlife including a large doe swimming across the river, with tiny spotted fawn twins trailing behind, swimming side by side in unison with just enough skill to keep their ears and noses out of the water.

Shortly after lunch we located the campground from the water, with Alcona Dam directly in front of us. Reading each other's minds, Angie and I knew that we could not stop to camp with a portage in sight and with the day only half done. We aimed for the dam, knowing by now that we could play the rest of the trip by ear. We decided to see how far we could get before dark.

Our technique for conquering a portage showed improvement. Fifteen minutes of shuttling took us from the portage step at the top of the dam to a fully loaded canoe ready to launch at the river below. The canoe was completely set and I was taking a well-deserved drink from my canteen when the sirens began to sound. The people fishing around the dam frantically began reeling in their lines. A man standing along the riverbank picked up his small son and ran for higher ground. We had to move fast, either pull our gear clear of the low streambed, or head for the middle of the stream and deal with the fast water when it came. Without hesitation Angie jumped into the front of the canoe and I heaved the craft into the current. We paddled with all our strength to get past the bridge footings in front of us and as far downstream as possible before the floodgates opened. As we passed the last footing, I glanced back to see a rush of new water coming from the foot of the dam and for the next few miles we were happy to have extra current to carry us along on our journey.

By 6:30 p.m. we found a beautiful single grassy campsite at the downstream end of Loud Dam Pond. We pitched our tent and watched the sun go down over the lake. It was then that Angie and I decided to make a final run for Lake Huron the next day, an effort well over thirty miles with four portages and at least twenty miles of currentless water. We agreed to be on the water at 6:30 a.m. and knew we would paddle until after dark if necessary.

When we crawled from our tent in the morning, a heavy fog covered the water. I wondered if the fog would thicken and prevent us from crossing the four lakes that we knew were ahead. It was an eerie feeling paddling through the mist with the water surface as smooth as glass and silent ripples cascading peacefully in concentric circles where our paddles entered the water.

We portaged the first dam at 6:45 a.m. and began a trek across Five Channels Dam Pond, a winding reservoir that is narrow enough to look as much like a river as a lake. By 9:00 a.m. we lowered the canoe into Cooke Dam Pond, the longest of the reservoirs. The fog was nearly gone. The early morning launch worked to our advantage, since we covered about two thirds of the still water before an east wind began to add resistance to our paddling. At 1:00 p.m. we lowered the canoe into the river feeding Foote Dam Pond with the wind blowing stiffly into our faces. When we turned the bend into the lake, we had whitecaps pounding against our bow. We paddled, inch by inch, knowing that if we could reach the dam the current would carry us the final distance to the mouth of the river. We crossed the lake by navigating from peninsula to peninsula. As we passed a landmark nearly half way across the lake, a powerboat charged past us, throwing even bigger waves in our direction. Before we could position the canoe to angle through the waves head on, they caught us from the side, throwing the vessel over a roller coaster of water with the wave crests crashing over the side of the canoe, leaving more than an inch of water on the canoe floor. With a sense of relief, at 3:00 p.m. we finally docked at Foote Dam Pond. We knew we were home free.

We began the lower portion of the Au Sable knowing that it would be important not to be off guard. Immediately we realized that this section of river was potentially more dangerous than any we had seen so far. Logs, driftwood and tree trunks lined the bed of the river, many of them an inch or less below the water surface. As Angie spotted obstacles over the bow, I steered around them.

Suddenly the front of the canoe began to rise out of the water. It slowed to a stop with the bow angled steeply in the air. We held our breath. We were sitting squarely on top of a tree trunk that had been cut off about one half inch below water level. The canoe was lined up perfectly with the current to keep us from tipping. With water more than six feet deep, we were like a car hanging over the edge of a cliff, waiting for a weight shift to topple us over the edge. We wiggled. The canoe shifted. We paddled backwards. No movement. We inched the canoe sideways. It began to spin. As the current pushed the back of the canoe downstream, we paddled backwards and broke free. I immediately spun the canoe bow back around in time to avoid broadsiding a similar obstruction just a few feet down river.

As we got closer to Oscoda, we began to see other canoes, out for a day's paddle. They bounced from shore to shore feeling their way down river. Angie and I paddled by each canoe, perfectly on course, coordinating our strokes like soldiers performing a drill. I knew those who watched us could not imagine where we had started, and the beaver dams we traversed over only five days earlier.

As we drifted under the US 23 highway bridge with traffic racing across it, I remembered how small and lonely the bridge at Frederic had been. We could see Lake Huron at the end of the huge break walls and we paddled alongside yachts and fishing charters as we made our way to the big lake. When we broke free of the river my heart felt satisfied. There was an endless shore of sand reaching out in both directions with a vast desert of water opening in front of us. We were part of it. We were out beyond the sand bars, out in the milky turquoise colored Great Lake. It was as if we had spent five days building up speed on the runway and were finally launched like a rocket into outer space.

We pointed our canoe to the south and paddled parallel to the shore until we recognized our hotel. Turning in toward shore, we pulled the canoe up on to the beach. When we stepped onto the sand, Angie walked towards me and raised her hand for a high five. At that moment I

imagined Angie might be the only ten-year-old to canoe the Au Sable River from its beginning to end in 1995. I wondered how many adults had actually started near Frederick and finished on
the shores of Lake Huron. I knew that we had together completed a remarkable expedition and that when Angie returned to school, her classmates would have trouble topping this one.

Chapter Three

Riding to Mackinac Island

Teamwork on a Tandem with a
Ten-Year-Old
A Ride Across Michigan

Lyla

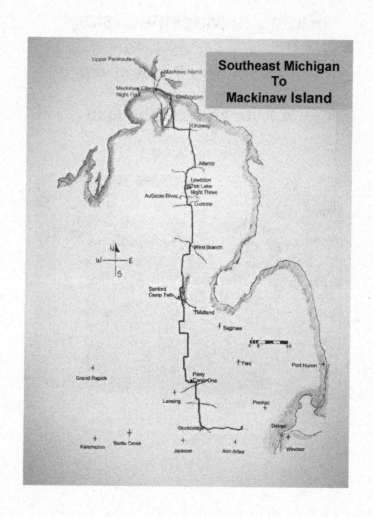

Southeast Michigan
To
Mackinaw Island

We had not planned to make a century ride. We certainly had not planned to make two century rides on consecutive days. Many adults would avoid a ride of 100 miles in a single day. For a ten-year-old, it might seem impossible!

It was the first week of August. Lyla had turned ten years old in January. For more than a year we planned to make a bike trip from our home, a small town near Ann Arbor, Michigan, to Mackinac Island, between Michigan's upper and lower peninsulas.

With the exception of a small training wheel type hand-me-down that Lyla had for a summer when she was six, she hadn't ridden a real two-wheeler until half way through her ninth year. A foreign assignment in India for the family put the bicycling part of Lyla's life on hold for a few years. But we always knew that this trip would be made in the summer of her tenth year. So, upon our return from this foreign land, one of the first items on the agenda was to find a suitable bike for Lyla.

I hadn't done any serious bicycling for more than twenty years. When I was in college my long-distance cycling consisted of a few one-day rides from Grand Rapids, back home to Farmington, near Detroit. My real bicycle touring happened in high school when I made numerous trips across the state with three other individuals. We camped along the way. My last bicycle trip to Mackinac Island was in 1974. It was one stop on a journey, as four of us, ages

14 to 16, circumnavigated Michigan's Lower Peninsula, and added a jaunt to Tahquamenon Falls in the Upper Peninsula. I remember this trip being nearly 1700 miles. Because of our age, we needed notes from our parents allowing us to stay alone in the state park campgrounds.

I still have my original Schwinn Continental and planned to ride it for the trip with Lyla. We began training in early June, riding seven to ten miles down the rural dirt roads each evening. By mid-June we dialed up the distance to nearly fifteen miles per practice run. Using a book of county maps, we started to plan our route, looking for a path that would break the trip into 75 to 85 mile segments, without adding extra miles for locating campgrounds. In early July I saw a car on the road with a tandem bicycle carried on its tailgate. As Lyla and I talked, we became enchanted with the idea of pedaling in unison on the trip. We began to look for a tandem.

Our visits to local bike shops taught us a few things. First, tandems are hard to find in July. The few local stores that carried tandems had sold their stock earlier in the spring. We also discovered that the price of a tandem might be prohibitive. The only tandem within twenty miles of our home, and available off the floor, was a beautiful Cannondale that was priced at double our budget. We tried to learn what we could about the technology and features of modern tandems. Our trip was less than three weeks away, including one week when I would be out of the country on business. We were still without a tandem. We looked harder.

As we searched, all recommendations pointed to the Continental Bike Shop, a no-frills establishment in Hazel Park, Michigan. The fact that there were tandems in stock made my heart beat a bit faster as I talked to John, the manager, on the phone. At noon that day I walked into the shop through what seemed to be a back door. I immediately saw a tandem leaning against the sales counter with a cardboard sign congratulating the couple who had set a new 24-hour tandem record of more than 440 miles on this bike just a few days earlier. I saw a crowded bulletin board with a snapshot of the record holders, as well as other bikes and riders who had done something extraordinary in their own way. I knew immediately that this was where we would find our cycle, and that we too would leave our mark on the small board at the back of this little shop.

I made my way between the bikes, and listened to John as he worked with a customer to find the right cycle. I realized that in the world of bikes, this man was no amateur. As he worked with me, he explained the technical and practical aspects of the tandems on his floor. We discussed the budget, the size constraints, and my long-term plan for the bike. We took a test ride together, my first on a modern tandem. He gave me a lesson about communication and teamwork on a tandem. Later that day, Lyla became the owner of a black, Burley Zyteco, 21-speed tandem weighing in at about 40 pounds.

I made arrangements to equip the bike with special tires that would be suitable for pavement and dirt roads, to exchange the front pedals, to add the back rack, panniers, a front pack, water bottles, a speedometer and a frame mounted pump. I planned to pick the bike up in two days, when I would surprise Lyla with, what John called, a new steed.

When I brought the bike home, we had only 8 days left that would work for training, three of which were weekend days. We pedaled fifteen miles the first day. The second day we made adjustments to the seats and handlebars. We added our full gear including sleeping bags, mats, a tent, loaded panniers, full packs, and a flag. We rode twenty-seven miles. On the third day we made additional adjustments to the bike and modified our method for packing the gear. We traveled fifteen miles. Each day we rode for at least an hour, and fine-tuned the arrangement of our gear.

With four days left until the trip, we bought cycling shorts because of the additional cushion they provided, rain gear with hopes that we would not have use for it, and cycling gloves with gel palms. Lyla and I were beginning to look like cyclists. To outfit ourselves, we added a sufficient supply of dehydrated food, energy bars, and stove fuel to our coffers. We reviewed our maps and made last minute route improvements. Our north bound route would take us on rural roads up the center of the state, where we would stay in campgrounds the first two nights, a friend's cottage on night three, finally reaching Mackinaw City on the fourth evening. Our distance projections were only roughly done, but we anticipated nothing more than 90 miles per day. We looked for stopping opportunities that might work for breakfast or lunch and marked them on the map. Duplicate maps were constructed, and would be left at home with Cathy and the other children so they could monitor our progress. Finally, we made hotel reservations in Mackinaw City, our anticipated reward for four days of pedaling.

On the evening of August 2, we carefully folded our clothes, gathered our cooking gear, restocked our first aid kit, reviewed our repair tools and spare parts supply and packed them into the empty compartments on the front and rear of the tandem. We placed three loaded water bottles in the refrigerator. Lyla said she would not be able to sleep as she climbed the stairs to her bedroom, thinking about our morning departure. I knew that if she waited for one day, she would have trouble staying awake.

It was 7:30 a.m. Tuesday morning. We stood behind the tandem waiting for Cathy to take a picture of our start. I reset the odometer. We straddled the bike. Lyla positioned the pedals. I counted down "three, two, one" and our legs began to move, peddling in unison as we quietly drifted down the driveway and onto the street. With a last look over our shoulders and a wave to those who would pick us up at the end of the week, we were soon out of sight.

Our goal for the first day was a campground near the town of Perry. We planned to ride in one-hour segments, with short rests between intervals. We hoped to find a store near the one-hour mark so we could top off our water bottles and polish off a Power Bar. The dirt road near our house led to North Territorial Road, where we began a westbound trek through the rural countryside toward the town of Stockbridge. The road was carrying some morning traffic of cars and trucks headed for US 23. They passed us cautiously in batches. The road was level but not wide. A pick-up truck honked twice as he approached. I thought to myself, "Are we going to be harassed like this for four days?" I looked in my mirror. He honked again. I gave the driver a mean look over my shoulder, only to see him pointing to the oversized section of a house being pulled on a trailer by the vehicle behind him. We immediately surrendered the side of the pavement. A good lesson was learned within the trip's first few minutes. This also proved to be the last horn we would hear until the ferry whistle indicated our departure across the Straits of Mackinac.

When we crossed US 23 a rolling terrain slowly emerged. The hills were short, but steep and frequent. We pedaled ambitiously from one hill to the next. When our first hour was complete, we had covered more than fifteen miles. These fifteen miles felt different from our practice runs. Upon its completion we were at the beginning of our ride rather than end. Our minds were focused on the horizon, and our bodies easily accepted the fact that we needed to repeat this distance four more times before calling it a day. We took the tandem from the tree it was leaning against, pointed it toward the west again, counted down the start and watched the miles disappear behind us.

North Territorial Road continued its aggressive terrain; one hill after another until ending at

Highway 52. This is a more developed road, with large paved shoulders and a human-made flatness about it. It carries a different breed of traffic including a concentration of trucks, traveling at higher speeds than those on North Territorial. From a bicycle's perspective, Highway 52 is an easy go. We played leapfrog on the shoulder with an electrical service truck inspecting the cables along the highway for nearly 10 miles. The route took a northeasterly trend into Stockbridge, where we happily sat down for an early lunch at McDonald's. We loaded ourselves with fast food burgers and several rounds of soft drinks and headed north with our sites on the intersection of Highway 52 and I-96.

A light wind blew in our faces as we traveled due north, but the sun was shining and we enjoyed the afternoon. After nearly fifteen miles of peddling the Zyteco coasted under I-96 and into the parking lot of another McDonald's near Webberville, stopping again for soft drinks and coffee. Continuing north on Highway 52, we quickly intersected Grand River Avenue at a spot I recognized from bike trips of my teen years. The two roads combined for a short westerly section until Highway 52 turned north again toward the small town of Perry. Our original plan was to take a road west before reaching Perry, and make camp at Moon Lake, which is situated about five miles southwest of the town. It was not clear which road the entrance to the campground was on, however, so we cycled into town to find someone who could provide us with information.

A cashier at the first gas station we encountered easily persuaded us that a more suitable campground was available. She suggested that we spend the night at Hickory Lake, where we were told there would be hot showers, a small lake for swimming, and a playground. Within an hour we had the tent pitched on a sunny lot next to the playground. Our odometer read 72 miles at the end of the first day. We had plenty of afternoon left to swim, hike and shower. It was early evening when Lyla finally reached deep into the saddlebags to find our camp stove and a package of dehydrated stew. The sun was going down when we climbed into the tent, expecting a good night's sleep.

At 11:30 p.m. the flash of distant lightning periodically masked the stars. By 1:00 a.m. the thunder was loud and the lightning not far off. The rain came in a downpour. We pulled everything away from the nylon walls. Lyla was only half awake and managed to drift towards

the center of the two-person Eureka tent. I repositioned the saddle bags and gear at the foot of the tent to bring them closer to the center, knowing that water could penetrate where there was contact with the tent wall, in spite of the excellent rain fly on the tent's exterior.

It was still raining lightly when the darkness of night began to disappear. We crawled out of the tent and managed to pack up most of the gear in dry condition. The sleeping bags were damp on the edges when we stuffed them into their sacks. When we pulled the mats from the tent they revealed a puddle on the tent floor, evidence that our efforts during the night were only partially effective. We packed up the tent, still wet, pulled on our rain gear and pedaled out of the campground before another soul was stirring.

The storm that blew in from the northwest during the night left the mile of dirt road for the campground a mess. Pedaling through the sandy mush made us happy to finally reach the pavement of Britton Road, which provided our path west for several miles. Its rolling hills were short and frequent, allowing us to glide down one side and sprint up the other. The rain was dripping off our helmet brims as we pushed hard to climb a steep incline from a low valley where the road crossed a creek. I heard a snap and felt the pedals slip from their normal cycle. Pedaling only a partial turn, I knew something had gone wrong. There was a quick shout from Lyla as she tried to plant her foot and found no support. When she looked up the scared expression on her face turned to tears. Her left pedal was laying on the ground behind her, and her leg was sore from hitting the cross bar.

Lyla held the bike as I picked up the pedal and reached into the front pack for our multi-tool. We went to work on the repair. The threads on the crank arm for the pedal were damaged from the incident and the shaft would not screw in by hand. Trying every option of the multi-tool, I discovered that this was probably the only fastener on the tandem that the tool was not suited to handle. Lyla placed the damaged pedal into the front pack and we headed down the road, powered by only three legs. The countryside was rural and there was no immediate help in sight. The task was doable, but our coordination reminded me of an injured horse, hobbling down its trail without with an unsymmetrical gait that only amplified its pain. Our Zyteco limped along like a wounded animal for three miles before an approaching vehicle stopped to take care of something along the roadside. The driver had no tools with her, but happily led us to a house nearby, and provided us with a crescent wrench to fix the pedal.

Before long we were back on the road, with a light rain pelting our faces. Five miles of northbound travel brought us into the small town of Laingsburg, where we found a hardware store and bought our missing wrench - a wrench that I hoped would not be needed during the remainder of our expedition. Not far from the hardware store a small restaurant was open for breakfast. We sat down for eggs and pancakes and were soon greeted by four serious cyclists.

"We were looking at your bike." One came to our table. "How long have you been on the road?"

"We started yesterday near Ann Arbor," Lyla offered, "We're riding to Mackinac Island."

The cyclist's eyebrows lifted high on his forehead. "How old are you?"

"Ten!" was the instant reply.

"Whoa, that's a long trip. We ride from Lansing to meet for breakfast at this restaurant every week. Hey Fred, come over here. These two are riding to Mackinac Island by themselves."

When we left the restaurant, we glanced at their bikes. Each had been custom assembled, using the latest technology with the lightest components. The peripheral attachments were the best available, but showed obvious signs of heavy use. The curiosity of these veteran cyclists flattered us as we mounted our fully loaded Zyteco and started north again.

Our course immediately intercepted Meridian Road, which we planned to ride due north for nearly seventy miles until we reached the town of Sanford. This route was nearly a straight line on the map. It rolled through Michigan's farm country with gentle hills adding the only variety to the terrain. We pedaled into a steady wind, which blew across the open fields without trees to resist it. We stopped in intervals of 15 miles for refreshment from our water bottles. There were certainly no McDonalds for coffee stops along this route. We encountered no filling stations, party stores or restaurants. Our only water and food were that carried with us. By mid-day Meridian Road intercepted the Gratiot - Saginaw State Game Area. To navigate around this obstacle, our path moved one mile east to Fenmore Road. The tandem was instantly wrestling a strong wind on a dirt road. At the first opportunity we moved back one mile to the west with hopes of regaining pavement. But when we finally stopped for lunch, we did so on the side of a gravel road. With the bike leaning against a boulder at the corner of a farmhouse yard, we pulled a loaf of bread from the panniers and put together peanut butter and jelly sandwiches. Power Bars capped off our rural picnic. With water running low, we knew that we must conserve what was left. The dirt roads continued.

When we reached Washington Road a farmer in the corner field was directing a tractor from row to row driven by his son. We laid the tandem on the ground and made our way through the crops to ask directions to the closest paved northbound road leading to Sanford.

"Well," the man began as he took time from his task, "just follow this road three miles to the west," he raised his arm and pointed the way, "till you come to Barry. That'll stay paved almost all the way to Sanford. A few miles up the road there'll be a store. You can get drinks there."

Lyla and I looked at each other with relief.

"If you stay on Meridian, you're in for eight more miles of gravel until it hits the main highway. That's alota dirt."

Lyla and I walked back to the bike and looked closely at our map. The new route would add six miles of cycling to the day. But it was all pavement. At the time, the extra distance and the chance of a store with a cool drink seemed a fair trade-off for a few additional miles.

We pedaled into a northwest wind until we reached the intersection of Barry Road. Our legs were tired and our water bottles empty as the tandem changed directions to the north. We needed the party store. As the bike moved slowly against the strong wind, we began to wonder if the pavement was worth the extra distance. Our speedometer read only 10 miles per hour, but we felt like we were giving an effort worth twice that. We struggled north, mile after mile until, after nearly an hour, far in the distance we could see a building with a row of colored triangular flags strung from the building to the road. We pedaled as if finishing the last mile of a marathon. Exhausted, the Zyteco and its passengers coasted through the small parking lot and came to rest next to the front door. The bike leaned wearily against the store's wall while we collapsed next to it, each absorbing a large container of Gatorade. Our odometer read 60 miles for the day and we knew that we must complete at least 27 more before setting up camp for the night.

The storekeeper suggested we change our route again for a more direct way into Sanford. At her advice we traveled directly east on Highway 46. In this direction the strong wind was at our back and we pedaled with new energy. Our speedometer read 22 miles per hour for three miles until we intercepted Meridian Road again. To the south we could see the gravel that we had avoided. We turned northbound, where new pavement began and pedaled until we approached the town of Sanford.

As the road made a broad bend into the town a vehicle pulled onto the shoulder in front of us. The driver motioned for us to stop. "I saw you riding and expected to see more of a group. Are you riding alone?"

"It's just the two of us." I replied. "We started near Ann Arbor two days ago and have been riding up the center of the state. Last night we were in Perry. We came up Meridian Road most of the way."

"Not a bad day's ride, but you could've picked a better route. You should have stayed on Barry, there's some new pavement that's really nice. We've got some good bike trails in the area too! Those sure are heavy duty tires you've got."

"They're special German tires made for a combination of pavement and gravel conditions." I didn't tell him why I was already glad that I had added them to the Zyteco for this trip. "You know, you're probably right about where we've ridden today. There's not much we can do about that now. What do you think about our route for tomorrow?"

The man looked over our plan. "I think you should be in good shape from here on. By the way, where are you having dinner? You should go to the Sanford Bar and Grill. It's up a few miles on your right. You'll have to ride a few miles past the campground, but you'll enjoy the food." He was a member of the Sanford bicycling organization, and asked if we needed anything for your tandem before saying goodbye.

It was about 6:00 p.m. when we pedaled into the parking lot of the Sanford Lake Bar and Grill. This didn't sound like a place to take a ten-year-old! But we each ordered a steak as a reward for a ride of almost 90 miles. A hot fudge sundae capped off the evening.

With one hour of daylight left, we mounted our tandem one more time for a three-mile jaunt to the Black Creek State Campground. There were many open sites. Lyla selected one close to the water pump. We unloaded the damp camping gear from our bike, hoping that there was still time for it to dry before we put it in place and crawled into the sleeping bags for the night. We leaned the fully assembled tent on one end of the picnic table, hoping its floor would dry. The sleeping bags hung from trees, and the rain fly was draped over a bush. The tandem needed minor adjustments to the rear seat height. We filled the water bottles, and finally moved the camping items into their proper location. It was well after dark when we entered the tent to settle in for the night. Lyla was sleeping almost immediately. At midnight a slight drizzle was filtering through the trees and gently striking the tent. By 1:00 a.m. the rain was coming down full force. By 1:30 a.m. the wind had picked up. The thunder was sounding and lightning flashes lit up the tent. Our gear wasn't as wet as I would have expected, but we were far from dry. With Lyla sleeping soundly, I spent the rest of the night in a half-awake state, listening to the rain and thinking about the day ahead.

At 6:00 a.m. the storm subsided and the sun began to lighten the sky. We crawled from our damp nylon cave and began to break camp, packing all of the belongings in wet condition.

There was no sense in trying to dry the gear with the rain dripping from the leaves above us. We dressed in our warmest clothes and made hot chocolate on our camp stove. By 7:00 a.m. the tandem was loaded and we were peddling out of the campground. We rode ten miles into Edenville where we intercepted northbound Route 30 and found a filling station with a small restaurant attached. Leaning the bike against the cinder block structure, we opened the screen door and slipped in for breakfast.

The restaurant had only four tables, a clue that we were in for some good local cooking. Our plates arrived overflowing with hash brown potatoes, scrambled eggs and toast. The men at the corner table were wearing plaid flannel shirts. Suspenders held up their Levis. While they filled the room with cigarette smoke, we could hear their conversation about tractor maintenance. We knew this was truly the flavor of rural Michigan. We wondered what these men would have thought if they knew where we had ridden from and where we were headed on a simple bicycle.

Along Route 30, we headed into a strong north wind. The landscape made a slow transition from pure farming land to forest and recreational communities. Lyla noticed that the chain linking the front and rear pedal sprockets was a bit loose. I would need to remember to tighten the chain in the evening when we reached our stopping place on Tee Lake. The road was nearly straight for 25 miles until it made a wide bend to the east in order to navigate around a number of small lakes. A convenience store and resale shop marked the turn's beginning. It was time to stop for a snack and something to drink. As I reached for my wallet, I noticed something unusual happening to my hands. They had an arthritic sort of stiffness and very little feeling in the fingers. I tried with little success to move my individual fingers. They worked better as a group than as single appendages. I tried to work some feeling back into the hands through simple exercise, and rubbing. It had little effect.

The storeowner was curious about our expedition. After reviewing the map, he suggested that at West Branch, rather than taking F7, we should travel east until we intercepted Highway 33. This would be a good road that would take us into Mio, where we could return southwest on Highway 72, in order to intercept our planned route at Luzerne. If we took F7 there would be about ten miles of gravel road in addition to several large hills, he thought. Highway 33 had hills also, but the road was paved. We thanked the storeowner for the information and were on our way.

As we pedaled, we considered our options. We planned to break for lunch in West Branch, a good size town that I now projected to be about 55 miles into our day. From there we could take our original route directly north on F7 for 25 miles to the small town of Luzerne, which appeared to be still 20 miles away from our destination near Lewiston. We expected to encounter some gravel and hills; pavement would begin again before we reached Luzerne. F7 would carry minimal traffic. The alternate route would add about 12 miles to the distance to Luzerne. It would be paved. We would still have to pedal up hills, though perhaps not as severe as on F7. Highway 33 would almost certainly have more opportunities for convenience stops along the way.

It was already 1:00 p.m. when we reached West Branch. The steady wind in our face had siphoned the energy from our bodies. Lyla and I leaned the tandem against the front wall of a pizza restaurant and dropped into two chairs inside. My hands were now functioning more like feet. The fingers would only bend in unison. The wait for pizza gave us a bit of recovery time as we absorbed several glasses of cola, and a few cups of coffee. We talked to the owner of the restaurant about the condition of F7. He said as the road left town we would encounter a very large hill, which would go on for several miles. F7 would remain paved for several more miles before turning to dirt for another 12 miles. The hills would not be so bad in the dirt section. When entering Oscoda County, the name of the road would change to 487. Somewhere in this area we could expect the pavement to begin.

Because of our experience the previous day we thought it would be best to maintain the direct route, not adding 12 miles of distance to avoid 12 miles of dirt roads. We mounted our tandem and headed due north on F7. The first hill leaving town was big. The second was bigger. We walked. When we reached the top and mounted the tandem again a passing car slowed and lowered their window.

"You rode all the way up that hill!" the driver shouted in amazement.

We didn't disagree.

The road continued on a general upward trend for several miles. It reached a plateau at an elevation considerably higher than West Branch, but the hills continued. The pavement ended. The tandem followed gravel road through the forest, over one hill after another. We rocketed down each hill in order to gain momentum to assist us up the next. I was truly thankful for the hybrid tires on these dirt roads. We were making good time. The forest broke the wind. The downward portion of the hills inspired us to pedal aggressively. We kept a keen eye on our odometer guessing at how much further until the paved surface. We walked two more hills.

Our odometer indicated that we had traveled 14 miles on gravel. There was no end in sight. The gravel changed to sand. Pedaling was unbelievably tough. Our bike zigzagged from one side of the road to the other in search of solid ground. Each turn of the pedal produced half a turn of slip. We pedaled hard for several miles, sometimes coming to a complete standstill and walking 100 yards before being able to continue. Hitting a pocket of sand along the left edge of the road, we put our full strength into the pedals, only to feel the main chain break free. The loose chain that Lyla had noticed earlier in the day was lying in the sand beneath the bike. It was coated with grit. Lyla reached into our front pack to find the tool kit. We used a towel to wipe the sand off the chain. Half of the priceless water from our last bottle was needed to help in the cleaning. My hands could barely work the Allen wrenches to loosen the eccentric at the front pedal bearings. I thought that this was probably what it would be like for an animal with paws to perform a bike repair. I reinstalled the chain, using the new open-end wrench we had acquired in Laingsburg and a rock to reposition the eccentric and set the proper chain tension.

We continued. Our rest during the breakdown gave us new life. The road didn't seem quite so sandy as it had been. After nearly 18 miles of gravel or sand road, with almost continuous hills, we finally reached a paved surface leading into the town of Luzerne. Travel on the pavement seemed to be no task at all, after the effort required to make the ride from West Branch to this spot. The tandem intercepted Highway 489 and glided into town.

At Luzerne we filled our water bottles and took a well-deserved break. Our plans were to meet some friends at their cottage near Lewiston for the night. I called Mark from the pay phone in Luzerne to let him know we were not far off.

"We'll meet you at the party store after the Parmalee Bridge," Mark said over the phone. "You know the place?"

We mounted the tandem and continued.

It was not long before a long hill sloped downwards bringing us to the Au Sable River. As we crossed the Parmalee Bridge I remembered four years earlier when Angie and I had camped at this spot during a trip down the Au Sable River by canoe. This was the spot where Angie's and Lyla's adventures intersected. We pedaled up the hill on the north side of the river to the party store and took a short break with hopes of seeing Mark. The remainder of the hill was extremely steep. We walked. As we mounted the tandem at the top, Mark's truck pulled up slowly from behind. His father, Dick, handed a much-appreciated cold beverage through the window. They had passed us while we were at the store without seeing the bike. We estimated one more hour of peddling before reaching their cottage. Mark and Dick drove off to prepare dinner. Lyla and I pedaled the final stretch for the day.

Taking a final turn onto the road leading to the cottage, Mark appeared on his bike to ride the last mile with us to the cottage. While approaching Tee Lake we discovered that the odometer was reading 99.5 miles. Lyla and I bypassed the cottage and rode for a few minutes longer. Finally stopping for the day, the odometer read 100.2 miles. It was Lyla's first century ride - a king size ride for a ten-year-old.

When we left the cabin the next morning, some of our gear stayed with Mark. Our next stop would be the northern tip of Michigan's lower peninsula and we had reservations at a hotel. There was no more need for the tent or stove, but sleeping bags would be necessary the following day when we planned to meet the rest of the family on Mackinac Island.

Mark prepared an early breakfast and wished us good luck as we pedaled off at 8:00 a.m. My hands had not improved with the night's rest. Simple tasks like tying shoelaces were nearly impossible. We pedaled north along Highway 489 as it wove around Little Wolf Lake and skirted the edge of Lewiston. After several miles the road intercepted Highway 491. Our tandem followed the northbound route, in a direction that would bring us to Route 32. The riding was pleasant as we made a general descent for nearly five miles along the country road. We knew that we had spent most of day three riding uphill, and expected that our final day would be a downward trend bringing us back to the elevation of the Great Lakes. In fact, things were not so simple. Our arrival at Route 32 was met with an aggressive uphill climb that caused us to walk for several hundred feet. As we took a short break at the top of the hill and surveyed the road ahead, it looked like a gentle roller coaster, with one hill after another ambling toward the town of Atlanta.

We rode on. In Atlanta Route 32 surrendered to a long northwesterly ride along Route 33. The road was excellent with enough pavement to make bicycle travel comfortable. The strongest head wind of our trip was fighting against us. Onaway, the next town of note, nearly 30 miles beyond Atlanta, seemed a reasonable destination for lunch. We pedaled into the wind. Our speedometer registered less than 9 miles per hour, but we pedaled with all our strength. Traveling north the hills had a slow relentless uphill trend that stretched for miles. We persisted into the heavy wind, one pedal after another. There was no opportunity to coast with the wind in our face. We longed for a small store to stop at for refreshment. After fifteen miles of pedaling, a roadside park provided a welcomed rest spot. It had been more than one and a half hours since our last break. We were feeling fatigued. We ate jerky from our pack and filled our empty water bottles at the well. We were not making good time, but Lyla was still in good spirits.

Pointing the tandem into the wind, we pedaled with what strength we had. After only a few miles the store we had been hoping for appeared. We took another break. Lyla's

hands were beginning to have problems similar to mine. I was concerned. As we sat exhausted next to the building a man in a truck pulled into the parking lot.

"Which direction did you come from?" he asked. "I just drove through the roadside park a few minutes ago. An old bear was there, big as life."

Lyla and I looked at each other with surprise, thinking about what we had only missed by minutes.

Resting at the store would have been an easy end for the day, but we were already having trouble maintaining the schedule that was necessary to complete our journey. We mounted the tandem and headed into the wind for another round. We struggled with every turn of the pedal. To distract ourselves we sang songs. This is the beauty of a tandem. While riding, the partners are close enough to talk. The hills continued. We pedaled until we could no more, walking what was left of each hill - pushing the tandem up the incline with hands that did not work. Our progress was bad. It was 1:00 p.m. and we had not eaten lunch yet. We had been on the road since 8:00 a.m. and had still not completed 50 miles. We persisted. Finally walking to the top of a hill at about 1:20 p.m. we saw the town of Onaway. Lyla and I mounted the tandem and pedaled to a small café in town.

Normally a lunch break would help us regain strength for the second half of the day. We discussed the situation. We must take the remainder of the day step by step. At Onaway the road makes a sharp turn to the west, maintaining that direction for at least 12 miles. This would take us out of the head wind for about an hour. Our plan was to coast down the hills, and walk up the hills if necessary. We would see how far we could make it. The terrain still needed to descend to the elevation of the Great Lakes. Looking at the map, it appeared that the descent would take place over about ten miles, which would give us another hour of easy riding. If we could make it at least to Cheboygan by the evening, a hotel would be close by. Later in the afternoon we would see how things would work out.

After nearly an hour of trying to eat lunch and rest, our appetites were gone and nearly half of each meal was left on each plate. We reviewed our maps one more time and pushed forward, knowing we were near the end of our

expedition, but not knowing if we could complete it today. It was 2:30 p.m. as we left the restaurant. Still exhausted, we coasted out of Onaway, cupping our hands over the bicycle handlebars because our fingers no longer worked. Highway 33 was heading due west. The hill out of town was a long slow descent, giving us at least two free miles. We were not fighting the wind and were pedaling with minimal effort. Our strength began to return slowly. As we came to an uphill run, Lyla stepped into the chore on the back of the tandem, powering us to the top. We coasted down another long descent. Lyla stood up and pedaled aggressively as we climbed the next hill. On the third hill we walked, each step bringing us closer to our goal. In one hour, we covered nearly twelve miles, our best time for the day, using less effort than required when traveling into the wind at only 8 miles per hour. When Highway 33 made a large bend to the north we hoped that the beginning of our descent to the Great Lakes elevation was near. We expected a few more hills but were beginning to feel as if we were had reached the home stretch. The road snaked around several more large hills and continued to roller coaster for nearly ten miles before dropping alongside Mullet Lake on a path that would bring us into the town of Cheboygan.

Before long we were in the town, navigating a stretch of road construction during a flurry of heavy traffic. We moved along with the cars, but with less elbowroom than on any other section of the trip. The traffic required us to keep pace in order to prevent cars from passing without ample room. Maintaining a strong speed of about 22 miles per hour for more than a mile, what we needed finally appeared on a busy corner - the Pizza Hut. It was 6:00 p.m. We could smell dinner cooking! There were about 17 miles left to reach the hotel. We knew we could make it.

Dinner seemed to give us our second wind. At 7:15 p.m. the tandem was back in motion, pedaling down US 23 along the shore of Lake Huron. The road was level and smooth, with a wide paved shoulder. Our direction was to the northwest, and the wind was not a factor. Our speedometer was holding steady at 16 miles per hour. As we traveled down the highway with the lakeshore to our right, we watched in amazement to see the Mackinac Bridge appear above the trees ahead. It was still miles off, but pedaling seemed effortless, and we felt triumphant as we glided down the final stretch. When we pulled into the Mill Creek Hotel at 8:30 p.m. our odometer read 101.2 miles - Lyla's second century ride in two days. The struggle of the day was behind us, and Lyla could boast like a champion that she had completed an event difficult for many adults. We had traveled 360 miles since we left home. I wondered if any other 10-year-old had made this trip during 1999.

When we registered at the hotel my fingers would not hold a pencil. I needed help from the hotel owner to push the buttons on the telephone. I had difficulty collecting change from my pocket. As things turned out, it took three weeks for my hands to recover. Lyla's recovered in one day. The hotel owners met us with hospitality and generosity. They gave us a personal tour of their facilities and Lake Huron beach. They drove us several miles to the grocery store so that we could buy snacks for the evening, and they listened with interest to our stories about the adventures along the way to Mackinaw City.

When the sun came up the following morning Lyla and I loaded our tandem again and rode to a spot for breakfast. We pedaled across the street and boarded a ferry to Mackinac Island where we would rendezvous with the rest of the family for two days of relaxation. I listened to the ferry whistle signal our departure from the shore. With our bike leaning against the rail of the boat we reflected on what we had just accomplished. There are probably better routes for cycling to the Straits of Mackinac. There may also be those who could make the trip in less than four days. But this trip stretched our personal abilities, and there are few people who would enjoy the ride any more than we did. We made the trip without a support crew to transport gear. We talked and sang for four days, instinctively experiencing a bonding teamwork while peddling. We set up a tent at night and felt the wind in our face during the day.

Now I watched as tourists boarded the ferry for a day on the island and wondered how many of them would make a trip in their lifetime that rivaled the adventure Lyla had just completed as a 10-year-old. I also knew that Lyla's picture had earned a spot on the board at the Continental Bike Shop.

Chapter Four

The North Channel

**Touring Lake Huron's North Channel
In a Kayak
With a Ten-Year-Old**

Kirk

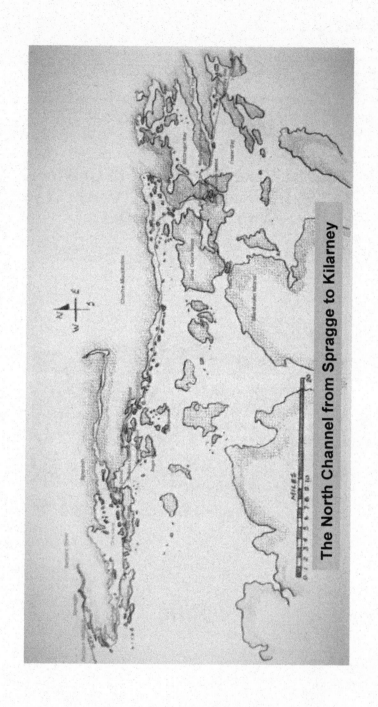

The North Channel from Spragge to Kilarney

When we slipped the kayak into the Serpent River the weather seemed mild. The kayak was loaded with camping provisions that would last five days. The river, with almost no current, was like glass and the dark water making its way slowly downstream was only half a mile from the river's mouth at Serpent Harbor, where the river empties into Lake Huron's North Channel.

This was only the second time that the tandem kayak had been wet; the same number of times Kirk and I had paddled this type of craft. We were novices to be sure, although I had spent plenty of time in a canoe. I had enough experience with long distance wilderness camping to prepare us for the wildness of the trip. But as we waved goodbye to the family from the launch at Spragge we were still breaking new ground.

I felt uncertain about turning a bend to the east in a few hours and exiting the protective cove of

Serpent Harbor. There, we would bring our eighteen-foot craft into bigger water; large enough to be called a Great Lake.

Our only experience in open seas was two hours of practice in Lake St. Clair. We had never faced waves six feet high, like the ones we heard could dance on the surface of the North Channel. From our trip on Lake St. Clair, we knew that we could expect to move at about four miles per hour. We had a basic feel for the paddles and rudder, but we had no experience with marine navigation. Our craft had a good compass bungeed to the deck in front of the rear cockpit. Our map cases on our deck bags contained charts 69 and 77 for Georgian Bay and the North Channel. We hoped these would be sufficient to guide us to where our car was waiting at Killarney, eighty miles away by water.

Kirk had celebrated his tenth birthday in June and knew that by mid-August we would take on a challenging adventure somewhere in the Great Lakes in a kayak. We were behind on planning. We looked at several locations in Michigan known for kayaking, but had trouble finding the right spot for the kind of trip we had in mind. Picture Rocks on the south shore of Lake Superior had rigid camping locations that did not allow for the daily distance flexibility we would need. Circumnavigating Isle Royale was too far for the time we had available. A friend familiar with pleasure boating recommended Lake Huron's North Channel. We found books, acquired charts, reviewed navigation software and settled on a route from Spragge to

Killarney; riddled with islands, bordered by mountains and peninsulas; with shorelines to guide us, open water stretches to challenge us, and unlimited flexibility for daily variation in distance or route.

Our Necky Amaruk kayak arrived, special order, at Venture Outdoors in Plymouth, Michigan in early July. We spent two weeks outfitting the boat with paddles, skirts for the cockpits, manual bilge pump, deck bags, compass, and several safety accessories. We found a small half-length wet suit for Kirk that provided warmth and buoyancy, and checked our life jackets and camping equipment.

During the first week of August, we made a final supply list and purchased the food. Our first attempt to pack the gear into the boat made us realize that, in addition to the space available in the front and rear hatches, we would need to bring a dry bag strapped to the rear deck. It took more experimentation with packing methods before finalizing our plan to put the majority of the food in the front compartment. We put clothes and hardware, such as water filter, stove, and mess kits in the rear compartment, and sleeping bags and tent in the dry bag. Sleeping mats were stowed behind each kayak seat.

The day finally arrived to strap the kayak on our vehicle and head for the water. Cathy drove our second van with three of our children to the northern part of Michigan where we would rendezvous later that night. I left our home several hours later, after picking up Angie, our oldest daughter, from camp and traveled with kayak and supplies to our meeting point at Lewiston. The following morning, we caravanned north across the Mackinac Bridge, through Sault St. Marie, into Ontario. We drove east along the north shore of Lake Huron until we arrived at the town of Killarney, where I parked and unloaded one vehicle. Kirk and I knew that our only means of retrieving the vehicle would be to complete our journey by water. We transferred the kayak and supplies to Cathy's van and backtracked for nearly three hours to the town of Espanola, where we had hotel reservations for the night.

Early the following morning the family departed from the hotel and traveled an hour west to Spragge, the beginning point for our kayak adventure. After thirty minutes of arranging gear, Kirk and I posed for a photo, slipped the kayak into the water and paddled a circle in the Serpent River, where a final photo could be taken of boat and crew before heading into our adventure. There were not likely to be other photographers along the way.

We synchronized our *Tail Wind* paddles while moving toward the river's mouth, each stroke quietly creating endless ripples on the smooth surface. With our rudder in the water a small line of bubbles trailed behind the boat. A pontoon boat made its way toward the river as we entered Serpent Harbour. We cut across the pontoon's wake and made for the south shore of the bay, skirted the rocky shore for two miles and tucked in behind Nobel Island, where our path narrowed to a thin channel for nearly another mile. We emerged from our secluded passage to see a small armada of anchored sailboats on the opposite shore, representing the North Channel Yacht Club.

The weather was blowing in as we continued a southeasterly course toward Long Point. Following the shore of the mainland, the Amaruk dodged small islands and peninsulas until we found a nice beach where we could take our first break. We had been traveling for more than an hour, and estimated our distance to be about four miles. To pace our eating, we each ate an apple, even though neither of us had an appetite. Gray skies were moving in from the southwest. When we lowered ourselves back into our kayak, a breeze blew in our faces, but the islands protected the water close to shore. We turned eastward after passing Gwynne Bay and noticed a single mast rising through the pines. A secluded cove lay hidden behind a small peninsula, perhaps a secret playground for a vacationing sailor. As our kayak swept around the bend, we found a large sailing craft anchored against the eastern shore in the company of two cabin cruisers. They had obviously laid claim to this gorgeous hide-away, so we raised a paddle to say hello and moved ahead through a beautiful narrow canyon bordering Long Point.

Coming from the opposite direction we encountered three of the sailors from the anchored vessel out for a joy ride in an inflatable dinghy. "How far have you come?" they asked. "We've only just started, but we hope to reach Killarney in a few days." Kirk replied with enthusiasm. They looked at our vessel, and gave a big smile to Kirk, as if they knew he was in for the time of his life. We had no idea that these would be the last humans we would talk to for three days.

When we left the water canyon and headed around Long Point the wind was blowing at us across the open water of the North Channel. This was our first feel for big water and the waves thrashed against the rocky shore throwing white splashes into the air as if they were backhanding the boulders. In the open water the waves reached about 18 inches as they churned about. We pointed our kayak east and decided to paddle one mile across the mouth of Taschereau Bay to Knight Point rather than follow the shoreline for nearly three miles. Crossing the bay, the water churned and we concentrated on keeping the boat upright. Several small islands dotted the seascape to our south. The chart told us that the water below was 77 feet deep.

The wind picked up as we reached Knights Point and we fought the waves close to shore, looking for a safe bay to beach for lunch. About one mile to the east, we pulled into a small cove providing some protection from the splashing. It was 1:00 p.m. and we had covered about eight miles since our 10:15 a.m. launch. We pulled the Amaruk onto the rocks and retrieved the makings for peanut butter and jelly sandwiches from the front hatch. Laying back on a boulder and staring at the clouds moving across the sky above us, I felt an inner tension from fighting the rough sea. I thought about the implicit trust that Kirk had in me for bringing him on this adventure and wondered what we would encounter along the way.

We continued along the mainland coast for several miles, watching the weather become increasingly gray until we entered Beardrop Harbour. The water in the harbor was perfectly calm due to the protection of a row of islands only several hundred yards offshore. Beyond the islands we could see a large mass of land that we presumed was John Island, a target we needed to reach as we proceeded southeast. Between John Island and the mainland, small islands peppered the water making up Whalesback Channel.

A light rain began to fall as we aimed for one small island after another, crossing the Whalesback. As the sprinkle seasoned the sea in front of us the churning motion of the waves diminished until we were gliding across open water, like a skate crossing fresh ice. Our path across the Whalesback was an angular trajectory of more than three miles. When we reached John Island we ducked into a small cove with a perfect sandy beach. It was late afternoon and we needed a break. The rain subsided and the softness of the sand that extended far out into the water was beckoning Kirk for a swim. He thrashed along the shore, waist deep in water, for a few minutes before knowing that we must move on in order to reach our destination for the day.

We traveled along the island's north coast with a natural protection from the southwest wind, across the North Channel. Skirting Davis Point, we took the short path across the bay's mouth. The rain started to fall again. Kirk watched our chart and crossed a small channel to Aikens Island, then to Rainboth and Klotz Islands. We navigated by keeping track of the islands we passed and the ones ahead that we could identify. It was getting late when we reached the west end of Aird Island. My left arm was cramped from the paddling. Every stroke tore at the muscles, which until then never seemed to have existed. We paddled due south into a cove at the first opportunity, a passage that separated Aird Island from Jackson Island. Our target for the evening had been roughly Jackson Island - we hoped to find a camping spot between Jackson and Aird Islands. We continued into the cove, first spotting reed beds along the west shore, hoping to locate a passage on the east shore that would bring us to our evening campsite. As we moved to the cove's end, we found nothing but reeds on all sides. A thin opening through the tall water-grass looked inviting. We paddled east into the foliage. The water shallowed until the kayak was beached, but we could see in the distance our harbor for the evening. With a sandy portage of less than twenty yards we were back in the water, looking at a promising small island one and a half miles ahead.

A light fog was rolling in as we paddled toward our destination. It made the island seem to move further from our reach as we approached. With each stroke of the paddle, my muscle felt like it would snap. As the fog got thicker and the island faded from our grasp, I began to use the paddle like a single canoe paddle to save my left arm. On the shore of Aird Island we passed a small cottage flying a Canadian flag, indicating that someone was home. We continued, chasing the gray outline of the rock that would be our campsite. Water dripped from our hats and noses; the air so thick that our kayak seemed to barely squeeze through it. The Amaruk slipped by several ancient logs lurking just below the surface, and came to rest on the rocky edge of the small piece of land. As Kirk searched for a suitable spot to pitch the tent, he could tell that others had chosen this spot before. Two large iron rings were imbedded in the rock on the island's west side, indicating an anchorage for yachts. We had made 23 miles the first day.

As I unloaded gear from the kayak, Kirk walked to the center of the island to explore our evening home. "Dad!" I heard, "an animal is watching me. I think it is a ferret maybe, but it could be bigger." I turned in time to see the black critter disappear into the dense brush that grew to

96

ankle level across the top of the island. How did this creature survive with this rock as its home? Here in our isolated hideout, we were only guests of the real owner, which we later concluded was a mink.

We put up the tent on a small shelf on the island's east side, with a cliff rising at our back and a steep drop to the water in front. Old pines canopied our site and we could see many more islands cropping up from the sea to the east. A ring of small stones set up to contain a campfire told us that others had been here before, who also took shelter in the shadow of this small cliff. We pulled cooking gear from the place it was stowed in our rear hatch and set out to prepare a few hot dogs on our camp stove. For the first night we had planned to eat fresh food rather than dehydrated selections. One of the advantages of traveling by kayak rather than foot is that carrying the weight of real food is not a problem. It had been a year since I last fired

97

up the backpacking stove, and I was not having much success keeping the flame lit. We could have made a wood fire from some of the scraps on the island but we wanted to stick to low impact camping, so we ate hotdogs cold, supplementing them with a can of sliced peaches and some pudding. By 9:00 p.m. our gear was neatly consolidated in the dry pack and we were lying on our backs in the tent, ready for sleep.

With a bit more energy in the morning I knew I must solve the problem of the stove. I searched its nylon case for a manual that I might have left there on an earlier trip. I inspected the stove more closely, looking for what could cause the fuel supply to the burner to repeatedly cut out. I discovered a small hole near the pump knob with an inscription marked "oil." For nearly ten years I had never oiled this spot, so I took the inscription as an instruction and dripped in some vegetable oil, the only oil we had on hand. Within a few minutes the pump seals had absorbed the lubricant and the fuel bottle nicely maintained the pressure necessary to supply the burner with a steady flow of stove gas.

Of course, having a working stove meant that I must perform as a breakfast cook. With pancakes on the menu, I may have been better off leaving the stove in its original condition. Kirk and I cautiously ate what should descriptively be called scrambled pancakes. We had hot chocolate and coffee and, I will admit, that the last pancake was round and flat and in one piece. Though we were no longer hungry, we felt we must eat the small creation just because it was so beautiful.

As I carried the dry pack to the boat, I realized that my arms would be a problem during the day's paddle. We stretched a bit and lowered ourselves into the cockpits for another journey eastward. The sun was shining and the air still. The smooth water invited us to glide across it. The paddle pulled at my left arm again, as we powered the craft forward. We took a slow methodical pace, following the shore of Aird Island. The waterway funneled us south of Passage Island, then Shanty Island, and finally, as we approached the east end of Aird Island, we could see Green Island further to our north.

At Arnold Point a peninsula from the main land snakes for several miles out into the water, stopping only yards from Arnold Point on Aird Island. Channel markers locate the narrow water passage between the two landmasses. The resulting channel, labeled Little Detroit, was obviously a well-traveled waterway. We saw several sailboats and pleasure craft traveling to and from the mainland town of Spanish on the North Shore. We imagined their destinations were the Benjamin Islands, or Little Current, or perhaps Killarney, where we might catch sight of them again a few days later.

As we approached Little Detroit, a lone kayaker followed the shore of the mainland through the channel in the distance. Our hope of meeting the other kayaker was fleeting since he followed the mainland shore north into Shoepack Bay.

Emerging from Little Detroit we set our rudder for the opposite direction. The weather was calm and we intended to cover four miles of open water with nearly no island to protect us from the waves. Our target was Eagle Island, and we hoped to dash across the open water, in some places 150 feet deep, in one hour while the weather was good. If the wind picked up, we would need to paddle about one mile south to a sparse row of tiny islands that seemed to lead to the same destination. Out in the open, knowing that there was no time to waste, we paddled with strong strokes. The pain in my arm disappeared as I concentrated on the crossing. Even with no wind, in the middle of the sea the swells were nearly 18 inches. But we now felt comfortable with these conditions and did not fight the sea with our paddles. We followed the path of a large sailboat perhaps a mile ahead of us, wondering if the sailors had spotted our insignificant vessel as it bobbed like a cork over the swells.

We passed south of Hiesordt Rocks; barren masses inhabited by seagulls, loons and other waterfowl. Several loons raised their wings and silhouetted themselves against the background, like oddly shaped scarecrows performing a yoga invented only to attract the curiosity of passing kayakers.

When we made Eagle Island the sun shone high in the sky and we began to look for a nice spot to have lunch. Frechette Island was to the northeast. Looking at the horizon to the southeast, we could see the Benjamins, a favorite spot for pleasure boaters. We pointed our bow to the north and tucked into a small channel between Hagarty and Frechette Islands. The North Channel was an island haven, rich with beautiful picnic spots. We beached the Amaruk for a noon meal in a picturesque cove off Hagarty Island near a large rock jutting into the water.

Peanut butter and jelly continued to be the big hit for Kirk. He used his new Swiss Army Knife to spread the fixings on the bread. Three sandwiches later we were lying on our backs on the rock, soaking in the sun and letting our feet cool in a natural crevasse that held a small pool of water left by tumbling waves.

It was nearly 2:00 p.m. when we coaxed ourselves back into motion. We estimated that we would need to travel at least seven more miles before making an early stop for the second night in a tent. Gliding along the north shore of Freschette Island, across McBean

Channel, we aimed for a passage between Oak Point on the mainland and Hotham Island. We were lured into the serene quietness of the secluded waterway's narrow entrance. A single mast rose from behind the shore to the west, telling of a secret cove with an anchored sailboat. My feet moved the rudder pedals for a turn to the east and we slipped along silently through the water as the land on either side closed in on us. The tall rocks lining the shore of Hotham Island projected straight down into the water creating a steep valley below the surface. As we paddled east, we noticed flagpoles rising through the trees, letting us know of the remote cabins we approached. We continued through the passage for three and a half miles until the island to our south gave way to a new and smaller stretch of land. Our kayak swept along the south shore of Anchor Island and through a narrow waterway adjacent to Lee Island. It was apparent that we were approaching some type of civilization. Flagpoles were more frequent and an occasional dock jutted out from the island. As we rounded the corner at McBean Harbor, there were cabins on both sides of us. The signs of life were two old cars parked on the mainland shore, and rowboats tied to docks on the island. Several hundred yards to our west a person lay sleeping in a lawn chair as a child walked across a porch without seeing us go by.

Half a mile ahead we could see Black Island, opposite Beaudry Point. We hoped this would be a suitable stopping place for the night. It was 4:00 p.m. and we had traveled 16 miles on the second day. We pulled up at a beach on a deserted smaller island just east of Black Island. I worked on the supplies while Kirk swam in the shallow water. We could hear children laughing nearly a mile away as they jumped from their dock into the water of McBean Harbor. Kirk commented "Isn't it nice to hear other children playing," wishing that he could join them for a few hours. He liked the security of seeing houses in the distance, and knowing that we were not entirely on our own.

The sky was still clear while I prepared for some culinary experimentation as a master chef in the wild. Kirk's unique eating habits reminded me of the ones I had when I was his age. One of my greatest concerns on the trip was keeping him from starvation. To that end we had planned the menu in detail and purchased the supplies together. Tonight's meal would push my cooking capabilities into a new realm as I concocted individual pizzas made of pita bread crusts, with sauce and mozzarella cheese. I used the frying pan with a lid as a makeshift oven. At first the heat was too low. The cheese did not melt, but the pita bread toasted. I turned up the heat until the cheese blended into a small puddle in the center of the first pizza waiting for just the right time to pull the cover. I turned my back to the stove only for a minute, and returned to billows of smoke pouring from under the cover of the pan. The pizza was done. Unfortunately, too done for Kirk. As I scraped the ingredients from frying pan, the burnt bread broke apart. Ah, crispy crust pizza! I asked Kirk to enjoy it and I repeated the recipe for myself.

To my palate, the meal worked, but Kirk managed to choke down only half of his pizza before surrendering to the peanut butter and jelly supplies; sandwich number eight in two days.

We pitched our tent on the beach that night, with the door opened to the setting sun. The weather had been perfect and we drifted to sleep, listening to the gentle lapping of calm surf against the rocks on the south side of the island.

As I normally do in the wild, I slept with one eye open. By 2:00 a.m. I became aware of the increasing noise of the surf and a cool breeze rustling through the branches of the poplars not far from our tent. Glancing through the tent's screen I could see no stars. Only a single light from a far-off cabin broke the darkness. The wind steadily picked up through the night. Before sunrise the waves were slapping against the rocks forty feet from our tent, sending white spray into the twilight air. The sun gradually broke the darkness, but only behind the cover of a low hanging blanket of gray clouds. Knowing that we would need to cover as much distance as we could while the conditions were still manageable, we ate a simple breakfast of dry cereal and packed up the supplies, still damp from the night's dew.

We were on the water by 8:00 a.m., a full hour and a half earlier than the previous day. This time we wore skirts over the open cockpits of the kayak to deflect the water we expected to encounter. We paddled through moderate waves across the open water to the mainland's shore. The wind direction had changed during the night and was blowing strongly into our faces as we follow the coast eastward. Today our arms felt ready for the challenge. We maintained a distance of only twenty feet from the shore as we paddled directly into the wind with waves easily two feet tall breaking against our bow. Our trusty Amaruk sliced through the surf without interruption as we slogged a steady pace with our paddles. The occasional wave broke over the hull of our craft, but the skirts kept us dry and warm. By 9:30 a.m. we were ready for a break. Having paddled only four miles, without protection of offshore islands we were traveling much slower than our intended rate. We slipped in behind a peninsula and beached the kayak on a marshy sandbar. The Cloche Mountains rose majestically from the shore ahead of us. We raided our supply of chocolates for a well-deserved treat.

Continuing eastward, our chart indicated that the next ten miles of shoreline was peppered with islands that would protect us from the large waves of the open channel. We welcomed the change. The wind was diminishing as we paddled from point to point, looking at the Cloche Mountains towering to the north. We came across isolated bays with long secluded shorelines containing the remnants of previously inhabited campsites. The water became calm enough to allow us to venture further from shore. From our vessel we could see cairns erected on rocks along the shore, the remnants from someone else's journey along this path. Our craft hopped from mainland to island as we paddled eastward, covering the distance at a reasonable pace with a light breeze in our faces. As we approached the east end of the chain of islands, we found ourselves trapped in a bay lined with reeds, rocks and trees. To retreat would mean adding about two miles to our day's paddle. As we neared the end

of the bay, we considered pulling through a field of water reeds, with hopes of portaging between the rocky mounds that separated us from the main waters of the North Channel. We pointed the kayak into the reeds and paddled on as if bushwhacking our way through a thick jungle. The water became shallower with each stroke. Nearing the end of the screen of reeds, Kirk saw open water, clear for passage between the rocks. A loud yelp signaled his delight and we clicked our paddles together on each side of the craft as a clap of approval.

When we emerged from cover a gentle wind was pushing at our back and the waves danced about as the wind changed directions from east to west. We followed happily along the shore with no protection from the wind and with waves cresting more than a foot high alongside the boat. We could see Great Cloche Island several miles to our south. As we paddled on, we noticed two other paddling vessels coming from an island offshore. They may have been half a mile south of us. Hungry for discussion, we paddled out to intercept them. As we approached, we realized that the crafts were canoes, navigating effortlessly over the increasing swells of the open water. Catching the lead canoe, we met Jan and Dave Heaven. We mentioned our surprise at meeting canoes so far from shore. They nodded as if it were nothing, and told us of their journey following nearly the same route as ours. Following behind, Sharon and John Rudolph paddled a beautiful wooden canoe. "Did you build that canoe?" I asked John as we paddled alongside.

"Now you've made his day!" shouted Jan from the front canoe. "Shall we pull up for lunch together?" Dave asked. With an affirmative nod Kirk and I pulled in behind our new leaders and watched with awe as they paddled their open craft across waves that exceeded two feet. Kirk and I took mental notes as we imitated the actions of these experienced canoeists.

Passing the first opportunity to beach on the mainland shore, we continued on with an increasing west wind at our back. Over his shoulder John said that if we didn't land soon his crew would mutiny! Dave and Jan led the way, passing by spots that were picturesque and open, looking for a small sandy beach that would be gentle on the hull of their beautiful canoes. With our polypropylene kayak, we hadn't even considered that factor. The paddling was easy with the wind at our back, and with no good spots along the shore, Dave headed out to a small island in the distance. We followed behind and before long all three crafts parked on a small sandy beach on this isolated island.

Our new friends were both retired couples from Hamilton, Ontario. The boat John piloted was 15 years old, and one of many he had built. These two couples were veterans of open water canoeing, already having several hundred-mile trips through Lake Superior under their belts. This was their second trip through the North Channel. They had been on the water two days longer than Kirk and I. Although they planned to pass through Killarney, their trip would continue on several more days along the shore of Georgian Bay.

As we ate lunch the wind picked up. Dave pointed across the water to Great Cloche Island and said "We were going to paddle to that island before we ran into you, but it's a bit further than we first thought." I looked at the huge waves plastering our island's shore and the whitecaps dancing along the crests. Great Cloche Island was more than four miles to our south, separated from us by only open water with the full force of the west wind pushing all of the North Channel's wave action into this mixing bowl in front of us.

"But," John said, "we have a rule that we never paddle in whitecaps." I nodded as if the rule made good sense but raised my eyebrows, looking across the water, seeing nothing but froth riding the top of each large wave. The wind continued to build.

We packed up the lunch supplies, and without further mention of whitecaps launched each boat individually into the turbulent seas. The wind was moving so fast that within minutes after Dave and Jan set out, they were almost uncatchable. John and Sharon launched next.

Kirk and I fastened down our skirts and pulled in behind John and Sharon as quickly as we could. We surfed from wave to wave with the thrill of a good roller coaster. We watched the canoes ahead of us handle the heavy seas with natural buoyancy. They frequently disappeared in the trough of a rogue wave. I held my breath expecting that their open craft would be swamped, only to see them float over the crest of the next whitecap. The first canoe finally held up in the protection of a small island, waiting for us to catch up. Wanting an experienced opinion, I asked John how large the waves had been that we had just surfed through. He estimated four and a half feet.

The wind at our back felt like a gift as we effortlessly maneuvered the vessel toward our destination and rolled through the water with waves crashing across our deck. We were entering the Bay of Islands, a section of our journey for which we had been unable to obtain a detailed chart. Fortunately, Dave had a map and guided us from island to island. In the distance we could see a water tower that identified a town on the east side of the La Cloche Channel, a water passage we would need to navigate through.

The three vessels pulled in from the rough sea to a glass-like cove created by a group of small islands. This was the spot where our new friends planned to camp for the night. It was only 4:00 p.m. We had already covered more distance than we had planned, due to help of the afternoon wind, and had more than made up the distance we had lost in the morning while paddling against the weather. Kirk and I were not so eager to give up this good fortune of a wind at our back. After thanking the two couples for their help and hospitality, we dug our paddles into the surface and pushed the kayak back out toward the rough water. When we emerged from shelter we could see a channel marker in the distance, and a choppy sea we must cross to get to it. With complete confidence after having navigated eight miles of rough white-capped water alongside of our canoe partners, we enjoyed the rolling ride of the southbound jaunt across the Bay of Islands. When we made the channel marker on the south shore we pulled up for a small break and removed the skirts from our cockpits.

Our forward course looked like a cakewalk, with a narrow channel making water so smooth that it perfectly reflected the image of the shore. We absorbed the pleasure of the peaceful paddling as we made a southbound course between the two landmasses. We knew that we could cover six miles to the next group of islands with the evening still young. After paddling half a mile, the channel opened to two large bays several miles wide. We hadn't expected the change and a strong wind was beginning to blow from the southwest. The waves were white-capped as we cut into them. Hugging the east shore, we were pelted by wave after wave. The ones that broke over the deck immediately dumped water into the cockpit. We paddled forward, ignoring the water sloshing around our legs. A large wave hit the bow and gave Kirk the shower he hadn't had in a few days.

We calmly slogged forward, getting closer to the south end of the bay, and looking for the bridge we had heard could be passed under. An occasional car traveled along the shore, but there was no sign of a bridge. Had we taken the wrong leg of the channel? Were we paddling into the wrong bay? We rested our paddles on the deck for a moment to consider the situation. We had nearly reached the end of this path and could see only a small structure and boat ramp on the shore. We paddled on, now only 50 feet from the shore. Our only option was to pull up on the beach, cross the road, and see if there was water on the other side. Perhaps a portage was possible. We aimed for a landing spot on the south shore. With only feet to go, a thin hidden passageway in the furthest southeast corner of the lake revealed a narrow channel under a series of hidden bridges. We clicked our paddles together in a triumphant salute and pushed the Amaruk forward into the shelter of the simple structures. Opening our deck bags, a well-deserved chocolate hit the spot.

It was nearly 6:00 p.m. and we pressed forward into calm water with a distinctly different flavor. Crossing under the road, we felt as if we were back in civilization. A rowboat with a small outboard zipped around the corner and dropped two of its three passengers off at a spot along the shore. We could see a number of cabins dotting the water's edge, each with poles flying the Canadian flag. This area is called Rainbow Country, suggesting a magical quality that descriptions can barely capture. The Amaruk followed the southern water passage and came around the edge of Birch Island. A row of small cabins appeared along the shore, and we knew that we had come upon a lodge. The kayak silently drifted next to a dock where one of the fishing guides asked if he could help us. We had traveled 28 miles since leaving our campsite near Black Island early that morning. We had eaten cold hot dogs, questionable pizza, and volumes of peanut butter and jelly sandwiches in three days. We asked for a room.

It wasn't long before Ingrid, the lodge host, strolled onto the dock and explained what was available. "We do have a cabin. The arrangements are American plan and dinner is about to be served. I think it's roast beef tonight. Would that be all right?" Ingrid didn't need to wait long for an answer. "The cabin is number

14. It has a shower. Why don't you pull your kayak around to this area where you can get it onto the shore? After you take a few minutes to get cleaned up, come on over to the main building and we'll set you down for dinner. We can sign you in after that's all done. By the way, where did you guys paddle from?"

"Well," we started, "that's a bit of a long story."

A shower never feels so good as it does after a few days of camping. Clean and hungry, we made our way to the main building. The walls of the dining room rated fairly high on my own Boone & Crocket scale of restaurant walls. Huge muskie, pike and bass decorated the room, each with plaques identifying the guests and guides who had bagged the lunkers. Large white tail racks peppered the wall between the fish mounts. Several groups were having dinner when we arrived. A number approached the table and asked, "Are you the ones who came in by kayak? We saw you pass our cabin. How long have you been on the water?" Our story circulated through the lodge quickly. The interest in our adventure made me feel welcomed. It made Kirk feel like a super-hero.

A sign hanging over the entrance door stating, "*You should have been here last week!*" We were just two of many adventurers passing through this lodge, each with a story to tell. We knew that our story might be the topic of a discussion when some new guest asks, "Did anything unusual happen here last week?"

At a lodge like this you can easily get to know other guests on a personal level. As it turns out, a number were from Ann Arbor, Pinckney, and Chelsea, all a stone's throw from our home in Michigan. One guest told me "We've been coming here for 30 years. You see that muskie over the fireplace? My grandpa caught that with a guide years ago." He walked over to see Ingrid and to buy his fishing license for the next day.

When the sun finally went down, Kirk crawled into a warm bed and I stood out on the cabin porch watching the lightning storm make fireworks across the eastern horizon. I wondered what the weather would be like tomorrow.

I woke before the sun was visible and saw the white remnant of a full moon hovering over the water. A low bank of pink clouds painted the sky at tree level and the few stars that were still visible were rapidly disappearing. The sky looked promising for the day, but a stiff wind blew from the north. Kirk opened his eyes as I was loading the dry pack for our last day on the water. He sat up on the bed and pulled on some warm clothes for breakfast at the lodge. While crossing the path to the dining room, a full rainbow crept across the sky, centered over the lodge as if to pinpoint the heart of Rainbow Country.

The comforts of lodge living, breakfast and coffee made our camping trip quite comfortable. The men from Pinckney who had purchased fishing licenses the previous night, finished their coffee and wished us a good trip on their way out. We finished breakfast, thanked the cook, and made our way again to our trusty tandem kayak. Some of the guests came to see us off. I reviewed our plan for crossing the water between McGregor Bay and Frazer Bay with one of the lodge guides. He advised us of the conditions we could expect and showed us where to pass from island to island if the seas were rough. With the strong wind we expected large waves at the crossing. We put the skirts over our cockpits and pushed the kayak into deeper water. Ingrid came to the dock as we were leaving, and the friends we had made waved goodbye as we turned our bow toward Killarney and followed the shore of Birch Island.

Before we reached the north end of Little La Cloche Island, we could see the stacks of the Canadian Cement Factory on the Shore of the La Cloche Peninsula. The channel between the peninsula and the island ends at the southern extreme of McGregor Bay. From a long distance we could see the small boat of our fishing friends bouncing around on the waves at the edge of the bay. By the time we reached the mouth of the channel, the small boat had pulled in close to the west shore and huge whitecaps were rolling toward our bow. The wind from the north was blowing fiercely across McGregor Bay and funneling violent wave action to the southern opening to Frazer Bay, the spot we must cross. We plunged into the mess, paddling northeast nearly into the wind. Our strategy was to hit the waves head-on until we had covered about half the open water, bringing us about half a mile further north than would have been required in a smooth crossing, then to spin the boat to a southeast direction where we could cut the waves at an angle and surf in behind a row of islands to the shore of McGregor Point. Our kayak pitched about, now facing the largest waves of the trip. Our confidence from having paddled more than 65 miles already through many conditions made us welcome the thrill of the rolling seas.

When we came about, we surfed like veterans toward our target on the east shore, skirting the south side of four small islands. Each provided a momentary break from the wild ride across the open wind-swept water. Coming around McGregor Point the waves were crashing into the rocks along the shore. There was nowhere to beach and wait for calmer times, but we would not have thought of doing so, since now we knew that our small craft would handle these seas like a champion.

When we made the turn and paddled east again, the water was calm near shore because of land blocking the wind from the north. Two miles ahead we could see the entrance to Baie Fine.   Sailboats were exiting the bay and clearing a prominent island before opening their sails for a morning of fun in windy Frazer Bay. We paddled to the island, and then to Frazer Point on the mainland where we took a shore break on the rocky beach. We were not far from another lodge flying a number of flags, and we could see cottages on islands and the mainland. The Killarney Ridge of the South La Cloche Range was to the north and a long peninsula called Bageley Point was across the bay to our south.

Our plan was to inspect Rat Portage at the east end of Frazer Bay to see whether we could cross the land, or whether we would need to add twelve miles to our day by navigating around the peninsula of Bageley Point. When we were about five miles from the portage the wind in Frazer Bay picked up and was blowing to the east. Rather than follow the shore, we set our rudder on a direct path to the portage and accepted the gift of a strong breeze at our back. The further we moved from shore the larger the waves we encountered, but we were never more than a mile from one shore or the other as we headed toward our destination.

As we neared the small bay at the entrance of Rat Portage, waves churned from every direction. They had all been forced to the end of the bay and fought chaotically for their chance to slap at the Amaruk. We ignored the assault, letting the last huge waves of our journey crash across the deck and slip off our skirts before retreating into the bay they had come from.

Kirk and I clicked our paddles together as we triumphantly pulled up on shore. The portage was marked only by Mother Nature. Two large hills gave way to a thin valley, the only place where the portage could have been. We considered the situation. The boat and gear must traverse several hundred feet uphill, over a small ridge, and then an equal distance downhill to a small inland lake. If we made the first step, we would see the conditions of another stretch of land on the far side of the lake upon arrival. Although rocks and roots lined the worn surface of the portage trail, the grass and leaves next to the trail looked smooth. Kirk was too small to handle the rear of the kayak, whether it was loaded or not. After a short discussion he convinced me that, under his supervision I could drag the craft, partially loaded, up the side of the trail. Kirk portaged the paddles. I yanked our boat with the rest of its load up the hill ten feet at a time. The polypropylene material of the kayak acted as an easy slide along the leaves and grass. I knew that our canoe friends, Dave, Jan, John and Sharon, would have cringed to see how we made this crossing. I cringed at what we were doing, thinking with reverence of the hand-crafted pieces of art that our friends paddled.

When we reached the small lake, I flipped the kayak on its side to inspect the bottom, and verified the indestructible feature I liked about the vessel.

We slipped the boat into the thin dark pool of water bordered by cliffs on both sides and with only a few strokes of the paddles Kirk had carried, glided to the far shore. The portage on the east side of the lake was much more civilized. Wide strips of rubber belting had been anchored to the ground to make a smooth surface for sliding a boat down to Killarney Bay. It was 1:30 p.m. and we had planned to have lunch at this spot. But with Killarney now visible, Kirk suggested that we make the final sprint for the finish line. Calm water of the bay made the crossing easy. We paddled with perfectly synchronized strokes as we passed powerboats and sailboats speeding out of Killarney Channel. We could see a forest of masts from yachts docked in the channel. As we learned to expect, by the time we reached the far shore, low clouds had blown in and we entered the channel from newly choppy seas.

Paddling through the center of the small town, our two-seater slipped unnoticed by the yachts ranging up to 70 feet long. Children riding water bicycles from dock to dock glanced a Kirk and may have imagined that he was out for a morning paddle in the bay with his father. When we reached the Killarney Mountain Lodge, the man tending the marina stepped out to show us where to pull the Kayak onto shore. Kirk and I raised our paddles high in the air for one last paddle click marking the end of our trip.

We were one day early for the reservations we had made and a room was not available. As we loaded the gear from the Amaruk back into the van and placed the craft on the roof, the man from the marina came to ask about our trip.

"That's a lot of gear you're packing. Where have you been?"

"Well, that's a bit of a long story," we started. A large grin hit his face as he looked at Kirk and considered that Kirk had just made the trip under paddle from Spragge.

"Aw," he sighed, "it's a shame that they don't have a spot for you tonight. Let's make a few phone calls." Within half an hour we had the last room at the Sportsman Inn at the opposite end of town. We thanked our helper and told him we would stop by to see him the next day when our reservations opened up.

Kirk and I sat in the bar at the Sportsman Inn and ordered lunch. Kirk asked for a grilled cheese sandwich and I ordered a hamburger. The waitress came back with a depressed look on her face. "The chef said he won't make a grilled cheese; can I get you a cheeseburger instead?"

As she looked at the sad expression on Kirk's face I said, "This young man has just paddled eighty miles in a kayak from the Serpent River. He's been looking forward to grilled cheese for two days. If grilled cheese isn't available, a cheeseburger will do."

The men at the table next to us heard the story. "Wow, you paddled from the Serpent River?"

one said to Kirk. "You know, when I was your age, my dad used to take me up here for an adventure. Now I take him!" He pointed to the older gentleman sitting next to him. "You know, in the old days when they had a cook here you could get a grilled cheese sandwich. Now that they have a chef, he won't make it for you. What do you make of that?"

The waitress pushed back the kitchen door and made her way to our table with soft drinks. "Well, Kirk," she said, "we can do grilled cheese after all, and I'm going to make it for you myself!" Kirk nearly cheered. An ear-to-ear grin erupted on his face.

The following day we checked into the Killarney Mountain Lodge in the early afternoon. We spent the day swimming in the pool, playing Ping-Pong and touring the shops in town. We ate lunch at Herbert Fisheries, Killarney's renowned spot for fish and chips. As we walked back to the lodge, our canoeing friends walked up from a dock. "We've come to check in on you!" they reported. "We've been asking around town. No one seemed to know of two people arriving in a yellow kayak. But we saw your boat from the water a few minutes ago and knew you were here." We spent half an hour catching up before Kirk handed them the line from the dock and watched them paddle on the second half of their journey.

That evening at the lodge we met a number of people, each having their own adventure, and each interested in ours. It was late when we finally said goodbye to a couple in the lounge who we spent the evening exchanging stories with. We slipped under the sheets of our warm beds. I closed my eyes, and hoped that when Kirk is older, he takes me back to the North Channel.

The Author

Dan Ellens and his wife, Cathy, live in southeast Michigan. Dan has been an outdoor enthusiast all his life. He is an accomplished wood carver and carpenter. Dan has hiked, canoed, camped, hunted and fished in Michigan since he was old enough to do so, as have Dan and Cathy's four children. Other titles by Dan include *A Time for India*, *Building the Bunkee – A Photo Anthology of Custom Log Cabin Building and One Man's Retirement Dream*, and *Treehouse Letters – The Unabridged Michigan Forest Life Journal*.

About *Turning Ten*
Great Adventures in the Great Lakes

The region defined by the Great Lakes is one of North America's premier locations for the amateur adventurer. It is a place where memories are made in abundance.

Turning Ten is a collection of accounts from four world-class outdoor adventures made by children with their father when they reached their tenth birthdays. These are stories of trips that would have been challenging for any adults. They are journeys that are doable by most teenagers. They are examples of how parents and children can bond as a team to reach challenging goals, with a guarantee of making lifelong memories in the process.